Grant Writing Boot Camp for Animal Advocates:

21 Lessons, 110 Boot Camp Tips, and 48 AI Pro Tips to Get You Funded

Grant Writing Boot Camp for Animal Advocates

21 Lessons, 110 Boot Camp Tips, and 48 AI Pro Tips to Help You Get Funded

By Cathy M. Rosenthal, CHES

Pet Pundit® Publishing

Grant Writing Boot Camp for Animal Advocates:
21 Lessons, 110 Boot Camp Tips, and 48 AI Pro Tips to Help You Get Funded

© 2025 Cathy M. Rosenthal

All rights reserved.

No part of this book may be reproduced, stored in a retrieval system, or transmitted in any form or by any means—electronic, mechanical, photocopying, recording, or otherwise—without the prior written permission of the publisher, except for brief quotations used in reviews or scholarly works.

Published by
Pet Pundit Publishing
Kerrville, Texas
www.cathyrosenthal.com

Front cover design by **Cathy M. Rosenthal**
Back cover design by **Evelina Garliauskiene**
Edited by **Jamie Canfield**
Interior layout and design by **Evelina Garliauskiene**

ISBN: 978-1-948-444-026
First Edition

For more resources, downloadable templates, and training materials, visit:
www.cathyrosenthal.com

CONTENTS

07		Acknowledgements
09		Introduction: Your Mission Deserves Funding – Let's Make That Happen
11		About Your Grant Writing Coach
12		How to Use this Book
15	**LESSON 1**	Getting Grant Ready: The 12 Essentials
31	**LESSON 2**	Finding the Right Funders: Matching Your Mission with the Right Money
43	**LESSON 3**	Your Grant Spreadsheet: Organizing Your Grants Like a Pro
47	**LESSON 4**	The Mission Statement and Organizational History: Highlighting Your History and Impact
53	**LESSON 5**	The Needs (or Problem) Statement: Building a Case for Why This Work Matters
57	**LESSON 6**	The Project Narrative: Turning Your Mission into Action
67	**LESSON 7**	Goals and Objectives: Showing Funders You Will Get Results
77	**LESSON 8**	Stories and Data: Crafting Proposals That Connect and Convince
83	**LESSON 9**	Target Audience and Demographics: Showing Funders Who You Serve
91	**LESSON 10**	Implementation Plan and Timelines: Proving to Funders You Can Deliver
101	**LESSON 11**	Evaluation and Metrics: Helping Funders See What Success Looks Like
109	**LESSON 12**	The Sustainability Question: Showing Funders Your Program Has Staying Power
115	**LESSON 13**	The Conclusion: What to Say When You've Said It All
119	**LESSON 14**	The Cover Letter: Framing Your Case
123	**LESSON 15**	Supporting Documents: Showcasing Your Readiness and Credibility
129	**LESSON 16**	Final Review: Proofing, Polishing, and Submitting Your Grant
135	**LESSON 17**	The Rejection: Understanding Why You Didn't Get Funded (and What to Do About It)
141	**LESSON 18**	Grant Implementation and Reporting Essentials: Keeping the Funder Informed (and Happy)
147	**LESSON 19**	Using AI in Grant Writing: Your Junior Writing Partner
151	**LESSON 20**	Beyond Grants: Diversifying your Funding Streams
161	**LESSON 21**	Being Mission Ready: Celebrating Your Graduation Day (Minus the Cap and Gown)
165	**A QUICK P.S.**	Share What You Learned, Write a Review, and Stay Connected
169	**APPENDIX 1**	How to Access Your All-in-One Grant Toolkit
171	**APPENDIX 2**	Links to the 110 Boot Camp Tips
177	**APPENDIX 3**	Links to the 48 AI Pro Tips
181	**APPENDIX 4**	Sample Grant

A grant is more than funding — it's a vote of confidence that your vision matters.

ACKNOWLEDGMENTS

A heartfelt thank you to **Jamie Canfield**, who edited this book with the perfect blend of clarity, kindness, and common sense. Your sharp eye and steady guidance helped shape this book into something stronger, smarter, and more useful. I'm grateful for your belief in this work—and in me.

To my designer, **Evelina Garliauskiene**—I feel incredibly fortunate to have found someone with the talent and vision to bring this book to life. Your eye for detail, creativity, and patience transformed my ideas into pages that are as beautiful as they are functional and easy to navigate.

Deep thanks to **Cliff Cullen** and **Jordan Craig** for being my early readers. Your honest feedback helped ensure every page of this book delivers something practical and powerful.

Thanks to my sisters, **Patty** and **Lorraine**, for always being a sounding board and for offering ideas that made this book stronger and more accessible for readers.

To my husband, **Stephen**—thank you for putting up with my odd working hours, for making me fabulous meals, and for taking such good care of me so I can write every day. You've given me the space, support, and love to do this work, and I couldn't have finished this book without you.

To everyone working in animal welfare: this book is for you. Thank you for showing up every day with compassion, creativity, and grit—even when the work is hard and the stakes are high. You show the world why this work matters.

And thank you to the animals for being our "why." You keep us going on the tough days, bring out our best on the good ones, and remind us of what's possible when compassion leads the way.

Because every grant written and program delivered brings us one step closer to a world where animals are safe, supported, and seen.

And that's the world we all want to live in.

INTRODUCTION

Your Mission Deserves Funding – Let's Make That Happen

Early in my career, I worked as a journalist and then as a copywriter at an advertising agency. They hired me to write radio ads, billboards, annual reports, press releases, direct mail campaigns—even the back of cereal boxes. (Back when we read cereal boxes at the breakfast table instead of scrolling through our smartphones.) It was all the classic marketing stuff.

There was just one problem: I had no idea how to write any of it. I knew how to write a newspaper story, but this type of writing was very different. It was tighter, more strategic, and honestly, a little intimidating. So, I did what most writers do when they're in over their heads: I went looking for a book to teach me how to do it.

That book was *The Copywriter's Handbook* by Robert Bly. I still have it. It's tattered, dog-eared, and filled with highlighter marks. For the first five years of my writing career, it sat on my desk and helped me figure how to write ads, brochures, and campaigns—one project at a time.

I learned because someone took the time to break it down, step by step. And that learning curve paid off. It helped me land my first public relations and marketing job at an animal shelter — and gave me the writing skills that made me valuable to the field all these decades.

Years later, when I started writing grants, though, there was no go-to book—at least not one written for animal advocates. So, I decided to create the book I wish I had when I got started in grant writing. One that passes forward everything I've learned in a way that's practical, approachable, and rooted in real-world experience.

That's exactly what I hope this book becomes for you—a resource you'll return to again and again as you build your grant writing skills, whether you're writing your very first proposal or your fiftieth. Because you're not just reading a book, you're stepping into a boot camp built specifically for animal welfare professionals. This is hands-on, real-world, step-by-step training—no theory, no fluff, no jargon.

Who are you? Maybe you're an executive director juggling a dozen other responsibilities in addition to grant writing. Maybe you're the communications or development staff member who suddenly has "grant writing" added to their plate—right between managing social media and resetting the Wi-Fi router. Maybe you're a grant writer already, but would like to learn more about what funders are really asking for? Or maybe you're a volunteer who wants to work for an animal group as a grant writer. (*Psst. After you complete this Boot Camp, write a sample grant for an animal organization's programs to show them you know what you're doing. Trust me, it makes a great impression.*)

Wherever you're starting from—this book is for you.

In this book, you'll learn how to:

- Identify funders who are a real match.
- Build proposals that answer funders' unspoken questions.
- Write with structure, clarity, and purpose.
- Set goals, measure outcomes, and report with confidence.
- Avoid common pitfalls that get good proposals rejected.

With built-in **Boot Camp Tips**, **AI Pro Tips**, practical examples, and a voice that speaks directly to the real challenges of animal nonprofits, this book is not just a how-to—it's a *what-funders-actually-want-to-see* manual.

And yes, we'll talk about artificial intelligence (AI). Lots of grant writers have worried that they will be replaced with AI. I can assure them they won't be replaced by AI, but they will be replaced by grant writers who don't know how to use AI to write better and faster. I'll show you how to use AI to brainstorm language, organize your thinking, clarify tricky sections, and make the process faster and more manageable. But no tool—not even AI—replaces your experience, your knowledge of your community, or your ability to tell your story with compassion. Because no matter how advanced technology becomes, your mission—the well-being of animals—remains the heart of the story.

I hope this book helps you find your voice, share your story, and secure the funding you need. Because when your programs succeed, animals and communities thrive—and that's the future we're building, one grant at a time.

Cathy M. Rosenthal, CHES
Workshops, Writing, and Coaching for Animal Welfare Advocates

ABOUT

Your Grant Writing Coach

Hi, I'm **Cathy M. Rosenthal**—and I've spent more than 35 years in animal welfare, working at every level in the field, from local shelters to national advocacy groups. Along the way, I've written grants that have brought in millions of dollars to help animals and the people who love them. I've also helped organizations turn good ideas into fundable programs that create real change in their communities.

But here's the thing: I didn't start out in fundraising. I started out as a professional photographer, then became a journalist, and later worked as an advertising copywriter before finally landing a job in the animal welfare field as a public relations director. That background taught me how to communicate clearly, connect with an audience, and persuade with purpose—skills that proved invaluable in animal welfare and grant writing.

Today, I help animal welfare groups across the country write stronger grants and annual reports, provide oversight on grant-funded projects, and train their teams in customer service and compassion fatigue. I also write a nationally syndicated pet column, speak at national conferences, and create humane education materials, including children's books about pets, which have been used in humane education programs across the U.S., Canada, and Puerto Rico.

Whether I'm writing grants, training teams, or creating content for kids and communities, my goal is the same: to strengthen the field of animal welfare and help more animals—and the people who care about them—thrive.

Because when animal advocates are equipped with the right tools, training, and funding, there's no limit to the good we can do.

Ways to Connect with Cathy:

- ☑ www.cathyrosenthal.com
- ☑ https://www.linkedin.com/in/cathyrosenthal/

HOW TO USE THIS BOOK

This book is a boot camp—coaching you step-by-step with the same kind of guidance you would get if I were sitting right beside you.

Every chapter walks you through the grant process, identifying your organization's needs, researching funders, writing stronger proposals, and managing the grant once it's awarded. You'll find both strategy and practical tools at every stage.

You don't have to read it cover to cover to start writing. Each chapter stands on its own and gives you exactly what you need, when you need it. So, feel free to jump ahead and dive into the lesson you want to learn right now. If you're working on a specific section—say, your **Needs Statement** or your **Objectives** and **Goals**—go directly to that chapter. And, whenever you see a **bolded word**, it signals that there's a lesson in the book covering that topic.

BOOT CAMP TIPS

When you see the **Boot Camp Tips** symbol, this is where you will find real-world advice from my decades of experience writing grants, managing projects, and coaching animal welfare professionals. These tips will help you avoid common mistakes and strengthen your proposals from day one.

AI PRO TIPS

When you see the **AI Pro Tips** symbol, these are tips that will show you how to use AI to save time, organize your thinking, refine your writing, and research funders—all while keeping your voice and mission front and center.

APPENDICES

At the end of this book, you'll find what you need to put what you've learned into action. You'll discover how to access my **All-in-One Grant Writing Toolkit**, plus links to every **Boot Camp Tip** and **AI Pro Tip**, all organized for easy reference when you need a quick refresher. You'll also find a **sample grant** that shows you exactly how to pull all the pieces together so that you can write with clarity and confidence.

Think of this book—and the companion site at **www.cathyrosenthal.com**—as a resource you'll come back to as your skills grow. Whether this is your first grant or your 50th, this book is built to be your personal grant-writing coach—guiding you step by step, cheering you on, and helping you stay focused on what matters most: funding the work that saves lives. Please use the book in whatever way serves you best.

You've got the mission.

You've got the passion.

Now, here are the skills you need for better grant writing.

Let's get started.

LESSON 1

Getting Grant Ready: The 12 Essentials

The biggest mistake animal welfare groups make is jumping into storytelling and grant writing before they know what story they need to tell. We love sharing the rescues, the happy adoptions, and the lives changed—and those stories matter. But if we don't get crystal clear on the specific need we're asking a funder to support, we risk writing a beautiful but irrelevant story that doesn't match the grant request.

This first lesson is about building that foundation first.

Great grants don't start with writing. They start with strategy. Step back and think before you begin. Every well-written grant starts by clearly identifying the need, the people involved, and the resources required. This isn't just about helping animals. It's about improving the system of care for pets, people, and the entire community.

Ask yourself:

- *What project do we need to launch, sustain, or expand?*
- *Who exactly are we trying to help, and how?*
- *What's stopping us from doing more?*
- *What specific resources are we missing? People, tools, money, materials?*
- *How does this need align with our overall mission and long-term goals?*

Answering these questions upfront helps clarify the purpose behind your proposal and keeps your writing grounded in real-world needs. It gives you the structure to move forward with intention, so when you do start writing, your story is aligned with the *"ask,"* not separate from it.

#1: *Create a digital folder.*
Before you start writing grants for the year, create a digital folder to store all your essentials. As we go, I'll show you what to add. You'll pull from this folder again and again throughout the year. Suggested subfolders should include:

- Your **Organization's History** to show the journey, the struggles, and the milestones that shaped who they are today.
- **Project Narratives** for each and every project you want money for.
- A **Story Bank** where staff can provide pictures and success stories for your grants.
- Project Budgets (one for each program or initiative).
- **Metrics** and **Data** (intake stats, ZIP code maps, outcome summaries).
- **Attachments** (501(c)3 letter, board list, staff bios, logo, budget, etc.).
- Past proposals (to repurpose or refine the language for future proposals).

Creating a digital folder helps you stay organized and reduces the panicked feeling that comes with approaching deadlines. It gives you a dedicated space to gather everything you need—documents, data, stories, and stats—so nothing gets lost in the shuffle.

Now, let's look at the **12 Essentials**—the things you absolutely need to do before you're ready to write your grant.

The 12 Essentials

Start with Need, Not Narrative

In animal welfare, we know who we're here for—the animals. But for funders, you have to connect the dots and show how helping animals also helps people and their communities.

Yes, sometimes the grant ask is about the animal, like an adoption program or a medical fund to help injured pets. But even then, it's never *just* about the pet. When you provide affordable vet care, you're easing financial stress for a family. When you find a home for a dog, you're giving someone emotional support, companionship, and stability. When you prevent parvovirus or distemper outbreaks, you're protecting public health and preventing disease outbreaks in shelters. Funders want to see that full picture.

This information is something we in animal welfare know instinctively, but funders don't always understand unless we spell it out for them. You must frame your work inside the bigger issues funders care about: public health and safety, family stability, access to services, equity, and neighborhood well-being.

Start by asking yourself: *What problem are we trying to solve?*

Are there too many stray animals in certain ZIP codes? Is there a lack of affordable veterinary care in some areas? The more specific you are, the stronger your grant will be. Funders respond to real, measurable needs—not vague statements like *"we need more support."*

Instead, say something like: *We need to hire a part-time outreach coordinator to expand our school-based humane education program to reach 5,000 students in the five ZIP codes responsible for 40% of our shelter's annual stray intake and owner surrenders.*

That's clear, targeted—and measurable.

#2: Define your need.
The clearer you define your need, the easier it is to write your entire proposal. A strong **Needs Statement** naturally leads to your goals, your budget, your outcomes, and even your evaluation plan. Nail this first, and everything else will fall into place.

#3: Avoid animal welfare lingo.
Funders may not know that TNR means *Trap-Neuter-Return* (or even what it involves), or that a community cat may also be a feral cat. Spell it out and make your language easy to understand.

Develop a Budget for Each Project

Think of your budget as the backbone of your proposal. It should clearly outline the costs tied to the work you're proposing—staff time, supplies, transportation, outreach materials, even overhead. A strong budget shows the funder you've done your homework and are ready to put their dollars to work efficiently.

Break down costs line by line, and if your project will have multiple stages (like surgeries, then transport program, then education rollouts), reflect that in the budget too. Try to anticipate all the expenses connected to your work, not just the obvious ones. And be transparent about how the money will be used.

#4: *Don't wait until a grant opens to start crunching numbers.*
The time to build your budget is *before* you're staring at a deadline. If you prepare your project budgets at the end of the calendar year as part of your annual planning, you'll be ready when grant season kicks in—and "future-you" will thank you.

#1: *Let AI be your editor.*
Once you build your draft budget, drop it into AI and ask: *"Review this budget for gaps or items I may have overlooked."* AI can help spot missing categories, catch duplication, or suggest refinements based on your project description. Use it like a second set of eyes.

Identify Your Clients and Target Audience

While animals are always at the heart of what we do, grants are typically written with people in mind. So, ask yourself: Who are the people we're helping by helping pets? Are they low-income pet owners in underserved areas? Seniors who rely on their pets for companionship? Neighborhoods with high stray populations and limited access to services? Define your audience and be specific. Funders want to know who benefits and why your organization is uniquely positioned to serve them.

For example, one day a clinic manager stepped outside to help an elderly woman load her recently neutered dog into her car, only to realize there was no car. The woman, 83 years old, had walked more than a mile with her dog in a wagon to get him to the clinic. No one knew until that moment. She didn't complain. She just wanted to do the right thing for her dog, and with no transportation, she said this was the only way she could do it.

That's exactly the kind of story funders need to hear. She *is* your target audience—the person your program was created to help. Her determination shows the real barriers many pet parents face, like lack of transportation, limited resources, and no easy way to access care. A transport program isn't just a nice addition, it's the bridge that makes care possible for people like her. And that's what funders want to invest in: Solutions that remove barriers and meet real needs.

#5: *Listen to your clients.*
Your clients are telling you—sometimes with words, sometimes with actions—exactly what services they need from your organization.

Assess Your Organization's Mission and Goals

We all love funding. But not all funding loves us back. Before you chase after a shiny grant, pause and ask: *Does this grant align with our work, or are we bending ourselves into a pretzel for money?*

Your project should align tightly with your mission. This may seem obvious, but it's easy to chase funding that sounds good, even if it doesn't quite fit. Funders appreciate organizations that stay mission-focused and don't chase every dollar.

#6: *Stay focused on mission, not money.*
Before you chase a grant, pause, and ask: *Does this project move us toward our long-term goals?* Will it help us grow in the right direction? If not, it may pull you off mission—and off track.

Review Past Performance and Projects

Funders don't fund dreams; they fund results. It's easy to say we want to help every pet in need. But funders are looking for something more specific: *"Show me how you've already made a difference, and how you'll build on that success."*

For example, maybe your spay/neuter program reduced the number of litters born in one neighborhood by 30% last year. That's the kind of clear, measurable progress that gets funders leaning forward.

Even your struggles tell a story if you can show how you adapted when something didn't work and what you learned for next time. Funders want to invest in organizations that are learning, improving, and demonstrating they can deliver results—not just hoping for the best.

#2: *Summarize your biggest program successes.*
Drop your program reports or past grant reports into AI and Prompt: *"Summarize our biggest program successes and outcomes over the last 12 months."* This can help you spot which stories or stats are strongest to highlight in upcoming grant proposals.

Build a Story Bank

Don't wait until a grant is due to scramble for a success story. Start building a story bank now. These are real examples of the people and pets your organization has helped—the ones that move funders from "interested" to "inspired." And trust me, if you don't write them down right away, they disappear faster than socks in a dryer. That amazing story you swore you would never forget? Gone by the end of the day.

Stories should include:

- Who was helped (e.g., a senior with a senior pet; a family who received emergency vet care).
- What challenge they faced.
- How your program made a difference.
- A quote or personal detail from the client that adds emotion.

You can use these stories in grant proposals, grant reports, newsletters, thank-you letters, donor appeals, and annual reports. The key is to collect them when they happen—not weeks later when the details have faded.

#7: *Make story collection a team sport.*
Everyone on your staff plays a role in grant success—not just the grant writer. If 20 staff members each submit just one story or case example per month, you'll have 240 real-life stories by year's end. Build this into staff meetings, case reviews, or monthly "story roundups." The more stories you collect, the more powerful your grant proposals become.

Talk to Your Stakeholders

Don't build your project in a vacuum. Talk with staff, board members, volunteers, community partners, clients—and yes, even potential funders. What are they seeing in the field? What ideas do they have for improvement? Including stakeholder feedback in your planning not only strengthens your project but shows funders you've done the work to build community support and collaboration.

For example, one spay/neuter clinic polled clients to ask what services they needed most. At the top of the list? Dental care and cleanings. Based on that input, the clinic pursued equipment grants to purchase a dental machine, an extra surgery table, and other essentials. Within the year, they expanded services to include dental cleanings. That kind of responsiveness not only meets real needs but demonstrates to funders that your work is grounded in direct community input and practical follow-through. Local grant funders especially appreciate groups who stay connected to their clients. Many funders enjoy meeting directly with grantees, visiting programs, and seeing how their dollars are making an impact. When you can show that your work is shaped by both client needs and stakeholder voices, it builds confidence that your organization is in tune with the community it serves.

Use Data to Support Your Project

Once you've gathered feedback from your stakeholders, it's time to back up what you've learned by pairing it with data and projects that directly drive your mission. Funders love stories, but they trust numbers. Your goal is to show that the problems you're addressing aren't just personal anecdotes—they reflect real, measurable needs in your community.

Start by asking questions like:

- *What problems do people face when it comes to pet care, pet retention, or public safety?*
- *Are there geographic areas with higher stray populations?*
- *Are there language barriers, transportation gaps, or income disparities limiting access to care?*
- *Are certain ZIP codes showing higher shelter intakes, dog bites, or owner surrenders?*

This is where your data earns its paycheck. Animal control reports, intake trends, census data, ZIP code mapping, and public health stats help move your proposal from "this feels important" to "here's why this matters right now."

If your team doesn't have the internal bandwidth to pull data, look for public sources, city government reports, or partnerships with universities and public health agencies. Even small data points can carry big weight when they align with your mission.

You're not just telling a story. You're showing funders your work is grounded in evidence. It's not, *"We believe this is a problem."* It is, *"Here's the proof. Let's solve it together."*

#8: *Show, don't tell.*
"We help animals everywhere" won't get you far. But *"42% of our stray intake comes from just 5 ZIP codes"*? Now you've got their attention. Funders want proof you can track success, so build your data early: surgeries performed, adoptions finalized, families reached. Measurable progress makes funders feel good about saying yes.

#9: *Pair Stories with Data.*
When you share a powerful client story, try to back it up with one related data point. *"We met Mrs. Rodriguez, who walked a mile with her dog in a wagon to reach our clinic. She's one of 700 pet owners in ZIP code 12345 without access to public transportation."* Funders love when the emotional meets the measurable. (We will take a deeper dive into this in *Lesson 8*, **Stories** and **Data**.)

#3: *Turn raw data into talking points.*
Once you've gathered intake numbers, census stats, or ZIP code maps, drop them into AI and prompt: *"Summarize the key themes and turn this into 2-3 sentences I can use in a grant proposal."* AI can help you translate raw data into clear, funder-friendly talking points.

Prioritize Your Programs

You may have ten great ideas, but funders want one clear, focused project to consider. If your proposal reads like a wish list, it's harder to fund. Funders want to know exactly where their dollars will make the most measurable difference.

To prioritize effectively, focus on the project that:

- Aligns closely with the funder's mission.

- Has clear goals and strong potential impact.
- Can show meaningful outcomes in a reasonable timeframe.
- Has a well-defined, realistic budget.
- Addresses current community needs and funding trends.

This is where internal conversations really matter. Bring in your leadership, program staff, or trusted partners to weigh the options. Look at past performance, evaluate your team's readiness, and choose the project that not only supports your mission, but gives the funder confidence you can deliver.

#10: *Start with what you are already doing.*
Look around you. Is there something you are already doing that works, but could go further with the right funding? Your strongest grants aren't always for brand-new ideas. They're for projects you already know make a difference.

#4: *Use AI to rank your projects.*
If you've got multiple project ideas, feed short summaries into AI and ask: *"Based on fundability and impact, rank these projects and explain why."* It won't replace your team's judgment, but it can spark helpful conversations.

Identify Resource Gaps

Every great project needs *resources* — people, tools, supplies, time — you name it. Be honest about what's missing to make the project work and show the funder exactly where their dollars will make the difference.

Maybe you need funding for a part-time outreach coordinator to knock on doors and talk with pet owners. Or a few tablets for field staff to enter data on the spot. Or gas money for the transport van that's crisscrossing your service area. These aren't "nice to haves" — they're the essential pieces that make the whole thing run.

Funders appreciate when you're upfront. You're not saying "We need money." You're saying, "Here's exactly how your grant helps us reach more animals and serve more people."

Having these answers before you start saves you hours of backtracking — and gives funders confidence you're ready to roll.

#11: Do a readiness check before you start writing the grant.
Before you start drafting your grant, gather your team for a quick gut check:

- *Do we have a solid, detailed budget?*
- *Do we have staff, partners, or volunteers ready to deliver?*
- *Are we collecting the kind of data funders will want in reports?*
- *Have we successfully delivered on past grants?*

Understand Grant Types

Before we get into types of grants you can seek, here's a quick reality check.

Many organizations assume grants will help them launch their organization and mission into the community. I often hear, *"We just need that first grant to get going."*

But here's the hard truth: most funders don't want to be your startup investor.

Funders generally look for organizations that are already up and running—typically for at least three years. They want to see that you've built some stability, hired staff (yes, all-volunteer organizations have a more difficult time getting grants), and have at least four active board members (who aren't all family members). They're not just funding your mission; they're funding your capacity to deliver based on your organization's stability.

That doesn't mean new groups or all-volunteer organizations can't get funding. Of course, you can! But most funders want to see a track record of consistency. They expect you to have a solid foundation in place before they will award a grant to an all-volunteer group. Demonstrating clear plans, reliable leadership, and even small successes can reassure funders that their investment will have lasting impact.

Funders usually classify grants into categories. If you don't know what kind of grant you're writing, you're likely to confuse your funder—or worse, get disqualified. Here are the most common types of grants:

▶ *General Operating Support:* These grants provide flexible dollars to cover day-to-day costs like rent, utilities, staff salaries, and basic operations. Often awarded to organizations with a proven track record and strong outcomes.

▶ *Program Support:* This is funding to run specific programs, and it's the most common grant type available. It supports well-defined programs like spay/neuter clinics, adoption events, vaccine clinics, or services for pet owners experiencing homelessness. Think of it as project-based funding with a clear beginning, middle, and end.

▶ *Capacity Building:* These grants help you grow stronger as an organization. This might mean staff training, upgrading technology, improving data systems, or investing in strategic planning. These funds strengthen your infrastructure so you can serve more animals (and people) more effectively.

▶ *Research:* These grants, while few, fund data collection and studies that help inform your work or evaluate impact. Useful when you're testing a new approach or trying to prove the effectiveness of an existing program.

▶ *Capital:* These grants are for renovations, expansions, new buildings, and vehicles or major equipment purchases. These are usually large, one-time investments in your physical infrastructure.

▶ *Seed Funding:* These grants are for start-up money for pilot programs or new ideas you want to test. They help you experiment, evaluate, and refine a concept before scaling it up. One group I know received a seed grant to lay the groundwork for increased access to care at their clinic. The funding helped them hire staff and purchase the equipment needed to launch the program. While the term may sound like it's meant for new organizations, seed funding is typically awarded to established groups with a solid track record — organizations ready to take the next step with a thoughtful, well-structured idea.

▶ *Collaborative:* These grants support projects that involve multiple partners working together toward a shared goal. Maybe you want to work with other organizations to bring humane education into schools or coordinate a mass spay/neuter campaign in an underserved area of town with several spay/neuter providers. Funders love seeing collaboration because shared resources can multiply impact in the community. Just be sure to clearly define each partner's roles and responsibilities.

▶ *Education:* Supports outreach, training, and public awareness campaigns. This could include humane education in schools, community workshops, or campaigns on pet care. (These grants aren't easy to find, but I wish they were. We definitely need more humane education out there.)

▶ *Community Development:* These grants support efforts that improve overall community well-being, which may often include multifaceted projects that connect pet owners with pet food, housing, vet care, or neighborhood revitalization. This could be a project that helps pets belonging to pet owners experiencing homelessness, or a transport program in an underserved community that increases access to care by bringing pets to a clinic for spay/neuter surgeries.

▶ *Equipment:* These grants are exactly what you expect—funds for tools, supplies or equipment that is essential to your work, like kennels, surgical packs, cat cages, dog beds, dog and cat toys, transport crates, or even IT equipment. These are often one-time grants to enhance or expand your capacity.

Each of these grant types supports a different kind of solution, but all of them work best when your project is clear, community-focused, and mission-aligned. (See the Boot Camp Sidebar in *Lesson 6* on *6 Tips for All-Volunteer Organizations* to help you frame an answer to a funder about the strength, structure, and sustainability of your volunteer group.)

#12: *Match your needs with the grant type.*
When you match your needs to a grant category, you improve your chances of success and make the reviewer's job easier. They can mentally sort your proposal into the right bucket, compare it to similar requests, and understand what success would look like.

#5: *Let AI help you research funders.*
If you're struggling to clarify your project needs, try listing out your ideas and asking AI to help you group them by grant category (e.g., capacity building, education, operating support, etc.). This can help you see more clearly where each project may fall and give you a head start when researching funders. You'll begin to notice patterns, like which projects fit common funding priorities, and which ones may be harder to place.

#6: *Draft short summaries for each project.*
You can also ask AI to help you draft short summaries for each project or generate a table of projected costs and outcomes—tools that can help your internal team prioritize what to pursue and make your grant planning more efficient. Think of AI not as a replacement for strategy but as a research assistant. It can help you organize your ideas, clarify your thinking, and cut down the time it takes to prepare strong, focused proposals.

Think Like a Funder

It's not just about finding funders who support animal work—it's about knowing exactly what kinds of grants they fund. Some only support general operating. Others fund specific programs. Some won't touch capital or equipment. And some are extremely niche—like funders who only support senior pets, or spay/neuter in rural counties, or disaster response. If you apply for the wrong type of funding, your proposal might get tossed before anyone even reads the second paragraph.

And here's another common trap: Don't twist yourself into knots trying to fit your program into a grant that isn't quite right. Funders can smell that desperation a mile away. A grant focused on disaster relief shouldn't be pitched as a way to fund your adoption program just because both "help animals." And that only weakens your proposal and hurts your future chances with that funder.

Always pause and ask yourself: *Would we do this work in this way even without this grant? If the answer is "probably not,"* it's time to rethink whether this grant is truly a fit.

Funders aren't ATM machines. They're partners. They want to invest in real change, not just fund another activity. They're reviewing your proposal through a very specific lens, asking themselves:

- *Why does this work matter right now?*
- *Who benefits, and how will you prove it?*
- *Can your team deliver?*
- *What's the risk? How are you managing it?*
- *Will the impact last after the grant ends?*
- *Does this project fit their board's priorities?*
- *Have you demonstrated results before?*

If you can answer those questions clearly up front, you've already done half the work of writing a winning proposal.

#13: *Develop your funding pitch.*
Summarize your grant project into one or two sentences to develop your funding pitch. It anchors your proposal, and helps you quickly assess your fit with a funder.

#7: Let AI help you spot weaknesses.
Paste your project summary into AI and ask it to act like a funder: *"Pretend you are a foundation program officer reviewing this proposal. What concerns or questions might you have after reading this grant?"* Let AI help you spot weaknesses—before your funder ever sees them.

LESSON 1 Key Takeaways

Identifying your needs is the foundation of every successful grant proposal. When you clearly define what you need, who you're helping, and how your work aligns with both your mission *and* your community's needs, you stop writing from a place of desperation—and start writing from a place of strategy.

Funders aren't just looking to help animals. They want to fund meaningful, lasting change. Your job is to connect your work to the real impact it has on both pets and people. When you understand your needs, you can better tell your story. *And that's what opens doors.*

Before you ever start writing your grant, have these things ready:

- ☑ *A clear description of the problem you're solving in one sentence.*
- ☑ *A draft budget that breaks down costs for this specific project.*
- ☑ *A defined target audience: who benefits, how, and why.*
- ☑ *A digital folder system started (story bank, attachments, budgets, data, proposals).*
- ☑ *One to two strong client or program stories that illustrate need and impact.*
- ☑ *A list of grant categories your project fits (operating, program, capacity, etc.).*
- ☑ *Notes on past program successes, outcomes, and lessons learned.*
- ☑ *Early input or ideas gathered from staff, clients, and community stakeholders.*
- ☑ *Community data (intake trends, stray data, census info, etc.) to back up the need.*
- ☑ *A prioritized project that's focused and ready for funding.*
- ☑ *A list of current resource gaps this grant could help fill.*

☑ *A one- to two-sentence "funding pitch" you can use to test funder fit.*

COMING UP NEXT In *Lesson 2,* we will explore how to find the **Right Funders** for your needs — not just any funder with a website and a deadline, but those who truly align with your mission.

Every proposal is a chance to teach someone new why your work matters; don't waste the opportunity.

NONPROFIT FUNDER

LESSON 2

Finding the Right Funders: Matching Your Mission with the Right Money

Finding funding is one of the biggest headaches—and biggest joys—in animal welfare. Some days you feel like a detective chasing down leads; other days you strike gold when the right funder says yes and you get to help more animals.

Whether you're trying to pay for more surgeries, expand your shelter's capacity, or launch a new outreach program, the key is knowing where to look, what kind of support funders offer, and how to evaluate whether a funder is a real match.

Where to Begin Your Search

- **Foundation Directory Online (FDO) (now a part of Candid):** Professional paid tool with thousands of private foundations searchable by subject, location, and funding type. fconline.foundationcenter.org
- **Instrumentl:** User-friendly, with free trials and paid tiers. Great filters by location, focus, and grant size. Especially helpful for tracking your pipeline. instrumentl.com
- **GrantStation:** Lists both private and government grant opportunities. Subscription-based. grantstation.com
- **Grant Gopher:** Low-cost option, great for small or grassroots groups. Searchable by state and category. grantgopher.com

#14: Match projects with the right funders.
Searching for funders can feel like walking into Costco—lots of options, easy to get overwhelmed, and tempting to leave with a shopping cart full of "maybe" funders you'll never pursue. Stay focused. Start with your clearest project need, and target funders who fit it.

#8: Not sure which grant platform is right for you?
Paste sample funders or grant descriptions into AI and ask it to compare features across FDO, Instrumentl, GrantStation, and Grant Gopher.

#9: Let AI save you time.
Drop a funder's mission statement or guidelines into AI and ask it to highlight key priorities or red flags.

#10: Let AI do the sorting.
If you have several grant ideas to consider, paste descriptions into AI and ask it to group them by type: operations, capital, outreach, etc. It's like having your own personal grant sorter.

- **Government Grants:** Federal opportunities for larger programs. Heavy on paperwork, but great for big-picture, regional impact. grants.gov

- **State & Local Government Sites:** Cities and counties may offer public health or community development grants that are often overlooked by animal groups.

#15: Subscribe to federal and state grant bulletins.
Visit Grants.gov and your state government sites. You would be surprised how many animal welfare-adjacent grants live in departments like public health, education, or safety.

- **Library Resources:** Many public libraries offer free access to the Foundation Directory Online site. Call ahead to ask. Bonus: some librarians will even help you run your search.

- **Local Banks & Credit Unions:** Watch for community reinvestment programs, charitable trusts, or sponsorships. Don't underestimate old-fashioned phone calls. Your best lead may not be listed online.

- **National Banks:** Many national banks oversee charitable foundations:
  - » Wells Fargo Philanthropy: wellsfargo.com/private-foundations
  - » JPMorgan Philanthropy: jpmorgan.com
  - » PNC Charitable Trust: pnc.com/philanthropy
  - » Bank of America Charitable Foundation: about.bankofamerica.com

- **Community Foundations:** These often hold dozens (or hundreds) of donor-advised funds (DAF) that give locally. (See Boot Camp Tip #25 for more information.) They're worth cultivating. One community foundation could lead to multiple funders.

- **Family Foundations and Trusts:** Often deeply personal and mission-driven. They may not have websites or public applications, but personal connections and referrals often open doors.

#16: Network with people who already support you.
Ask your board, volunteers, and donors where they work or who they know. Someone may have a connection to a family fund or donor-advised fund just waiting for a personal introduction.

- **Humane-Focused National Funders:** ASPCA, Banfield Foundation, Best Friends, Maddie's Fund, Petco Love, Petfinder Foundation, PetSmart Charities, and more. These are your most animal-welfare-specific players.

#17: Relationships build grants long before you apply.
Strong grants often grow out of strong relationships. Even if you're not ready to apply this year, follow the funder's work on social media, join webinars they host, or sign up for their newsletters. That "warm intro" could make a huge difference when you're ready to submit. Keep track of who you contact and when you meet with them. A "no" today may be a "yes" tomorrow.

#18: *Don't overlook corporate funders in your own backyard.*
Some of your best funders may be hiding in plain sight—local employers where your board, volunteers, or donors already work. This isn't just sponsorship territory. Many mid-size and large businesses in your area may have grant programs, employee giving, or corporate philanthropy funds set aside for local causes. Talk to your board, volunteers, donors, friends, and family. Ask:

- *Does your company offer employee giving or donation match programs?*
- *Can you nominate a charity for company grants?*
- *Do they provide staff volunteers for community events?*

You may uncover both funding and your next volunteer crew for that 5K fun run or pet vaccine clinic—all by simply asking the people already closest to your mission if the companies they work for are philanthropic.

Follow the Money: What in Candid Can Reveal About Funders

One of the best tools you can use during the research phase of grant writing is Candid (formerly GuideStar). Candid is a free online database that provides detailed information on nonprofit organizations and foundations, including their publicly filed IRS Form 990s. It's one of the fastest ways to peek inside a funder's giving history, financials, and priorities.

Here's how Candid can help you:

- Search for foundations and view their 990 tax returns.
- See who they've funded over the past few years, including the names of nonprofits, the amounts granted, and general categories like "program support," "general operating," or "capacity building."
- Estimate the average grant size to organizations like yours.
- Identify giving trends and consistency over multiple years.
- Look up board member names to find potential connections.
- Review large or unusual grants that signal new priorities or capital campaign potential.

You won't always see the exact project details, but you'll get a sense of what the foundation supports. For example, if you see that local animal shelters received around $35,000 last year and spay/neuter clinics received about $20,000, you'll have a ballpark idea of what a reasonable grant request for your organization might be.

If you notice one organization received a much larger amount, however, say, $100,000 or more, it likely indicates the foundation supported a capital campaign or a major initiative.

That may indicate the foundation sees themselves as shaping the future of animal welfare and is open to larger-scale or game-changing projects. But don't expect that kind of giving year after year.

Use this intel to:
- Set a realistic grant request amount.
- See where your organization fits into the funding landscape.
- Identify foundations open to animal welfare causes.
- Spot potential relationships or introductions via board members.

Candid is a simple but powerful way to make your grant strategy smarter.

#19: *Size your ask strategically.*
Don't scare off funders (or waste your own time) by asking for the wrong amount. Your first ask shouldn't be $50,000—unless that's the funder's minimum grant. And if you're a $6 million organization, you probably don't need to be chasing $1,000 or $5,000 grants.

The goal is to produce a right-sized, respectful ask that feels like a win-win for you and for the funder.

Stay in the sweet spot:
- **Aim** just below a funder's average grant size, especially on your first request.
- **Leave** the smallest grants to smaller groups who truly need that early-stage support.
- **Consider** how your budget size and reserves will look to the funder. They are often quietly asking themselves: *Will my grant make a difference here?* If the answer feels like "no," they move on.

#11: *Turn tax forms into actionable intelligence.*
Once you download a 990 form, paste the organization's giving history into an AI tool and ask it to summarize trends, average grant sizes, and potential alignment with your mission.

You can also ask it to compare multiple funders or extract board names. This can help you decide quickly whether a funder is worth pursuing and streamline your outreach.

Aligning Your Needs with the Right Foundation

Submitting a grant to the wrong funder is like applying for a job in a field you've never worked in. Sure, you love animals, but that doesn't qualify you to apply for a marine biology research grant just because it involves fish.

Funders aren't just looking for polished proposals; they're looking for alignment. They want to support work that fits their mission, priorities, and funding capacity.

Before you apply, take a close look at the funder's history. What types of organizations have they supported? What projects do they seem to prioritize? What's their average gift size? These clues help you determine whether your work is a natural fit—or a long shot.

#20: *When in doubt, ask the funder.*
If you're unsure about alignment, reach out. Many funders welcome brief inquiries. A quick email or phone call can confirm whether your project fits their priorities—and shows you're serious and respectful of their time.

#21: *Write a one-sentence alignment test before you begin.*
"This funder supports _____ and we're requesting _____ to do _____."

Geographic Location: Many foundations limit giving to specific regions—sometimes a single city, county, or state. A local foundation might only fund programs within Harris County, for example. If your rescue is just outside that boundary, your proposal won't likely be considered—no matter how great it is. Before you do anything else, make sure your organization falls within their geographical funding area.

#22: *Double-check their geographic funding area.*
Check their grant website or one of the grant search tools to verify their geographic giving area. If you notice they claim to fund only Texas groups but have also given to organizations in Florida or New York, it likely reflects trustee influence or board members directing one-time gifts—not a trend you can count on.

#12: *Use AI to spot geographic patterns.*
Unsure if your location fits? Paste a list of a foundation's past grantees into AI and ask it to identify location patterns (e.g., counties, cities, ZIP codes). This helps you avoid wasting time on funders unlikely to consider your region.

Amount Funded: Every foundation has a general range they typically give. If your request is far above or below that range, it can signal a mismatch. Scale your ask to match their giving history or split a big project into smaller, fundable phases.

#23: *Check average grant sizes before you determine your ask.*
Use the funder's 990 forms or website to research their typical grant amounts. When looking at 990s, review multiple years to spot patterns and avoid basing your request on an unusually large or small one-time gift.

Types of Grants Funded: Some funders love to support new programs. Others only fund capital projects or general operating support. Make sure your request aligns with what they actually fund. If your spay/neuter clinic needs new surgical equipment, don't apply to a foundation that only funds general operating or project grants. Look for one that supports equipment.

#24: *Past giving tells you what the funder really supports.*
Don't stop at what the funder says they will fund—look at where their money has actually gone. Their grant history tells you what they truly care about.
- Seeing lots of shelters, spay/neuter, or TNR groups? You're likely in the right place.
- Seeing mostly wildlife or land conservation? That's probably not your lane—unless, of course, your shelter also runs a wildlife rehab program (then you've got a connection).
- The more you study their real giving history, the more time you'll save chasing funders who were never a fit in the first place.

#25: *Dig into part XV of the 990 for funder priorities.*
You can find a foundation's giving history in *Part XV: Grants and Contributions Paid During the Year* of their 990 forms (sometimes called *Schedule I* for larger organizations).

This section lists who received grants, how much they received, and sometimes a very short project description. Smaller family foundations may sometimes redact or omit full recipient details when filing. Some use donor-advised funds (DAFs)—charitable giving accounts that allow individual donors to recommend grants to nonprofits through a sponsoring organization, making it harder to see what monies were given that year. Because the sponsoring organization technically controls the funds, it can be harder to trace where the money came from or why it was granted. But most of the time, especially with traditional private foundations, this section gives you a great peek into their real funding priorities.

You won't see long explanations, but you *will* see who got how much and what type of grant it was—general operating, program, etc. and that's gold when you're trying to size your ask and assess alignment.

#26: Don't miss deadlines.
Timing matters. Some foundations accept applications year-round, while others have strict deadlines—sometimes just once a year.

Missing a deadline can mean waiting another 12 months for another shot. And if you've ever discovered a deadline was today, not next week, you know the unique panic of trying to write a coherent, compelling grant while running on coffee, adrenaline, and the hope that spellcheck catches everything. Don't be that person. A deadline calendar is your best friend.

What Seasoned Grant Writers Ask

These are the same questions seasoned grant writers ask themselves before they begin writing. Use them to sharpen your focus and reduce wasted effort.

- **What do we need and why?**
  Get specific. Why now? Who benefits? Example: *"We need $15,000 to expand our spay/neuter services into ZIP 75115 where we've seen a 40% increase in calls to animal care services regarding stray dogs on the street."*

- **How does this project align with our mission and goals?**
  Is it in your strategic plan? Is it core to your mission?

- **Who will this project help?**
  Always bring the impact back to people.
  Example: "Sterilizing 250 community cats also supports low-income community cat caregivers and improves public health."

- **Do we have the staff, space, and systems to manage this project well?**
  Be honest about internal capacity.

- **Can we meet reporting or matching requirements?**
  Budget thoroughly. Understand what's expected post-award.

- **Have we reviewed this funder's priorities, history, and requirements?**
  Align your proposal with their actual giving, not just their stated interests.

- **Can we meet the application deadline and reporting expectations?**
  Rushed grants are weak grants. Give yourself time to write a great grant proposal.

- **Are we submitting this grant because it's a good fit—or because we're desperate?**
  Stay focused on strategic alignment.

#13: *Use AI to reframe your ask through a funder's eyes.*
Try writing out your project's need in one paragraph and ask AI to reframe it from a funder's perspective. It can help you clarify your ask and strengthen your narrative.

#14: *Let AI sort and prioritize your funder list.*
If you keep your funder research in a spreadsheet, you can paste your top entries into AI and ask it to sort by best-fit funders, summarize deadlines, or recommend your top three based on criteria like alignment, giving size, and past giving trends. This can help you make confident choices faster—especially when deadlines are tight.

#15: *Ask AI for a second opinion.*
Found a funder you *think* is a match but aren't sure? Paste in their mission statement, grant guidelines, and a paragraph about your project. Then ask AI: *"Based on this funder's priorities, would this project be a good fit? What potential red flags or alignment issues do you see?"* This gives you an objective second opinion before investing hours in writing.

#16: *Speed up your research with AI summaries and comparisons.*
You can also use AI tools to speed up your research. For example, you can copy and paste text from a funder's website into an AI tool and ask it to summarize the key information: what they fund, where they fund, typical grant sizes, and whether your project might be a match. You can also ask AI to compare multiple funders side by side or compile a list of funders based on keywords related to your mission. This can save hours of research time, especially if you're juggling multiple deadlines. If you're new to using AI this way, don't worry. Start small, experiment, and you'll quickly build confidence in how to make it work for you.

#17: *Use AI to summarize key dates from 990 forms.*
Once you download a funder's 990, paste sections into AI and ask for summaries, like average grant size, top grantees, or funding priorities. This is an easy way to speed up your funder research.

#18: Use AI to run a funder risk check.
Ask AI, "Review this foundation's last three 990s and tell me: (1) whether they fund the same organizations year after year, (2) if their total giving is growing or shrinking, and (3) any red flags, such as one-time grants or big drops in revenue, that might make them a less reliable prospect."

#27: Create a "No for Now" folder.
Not every funder will be a fit, but that doesn't mean you won't ever line up. If you find funders who align well but don't currently have open applications, save them in a folder with a reminder to check again in six months.

#28: Budget time in YOUR schedule for grant prospecting.
Researching funders takes time—and it's real work. Block 2 to 4 hours per week for discovery and alignment review. As you work, you'll start building a solid funder research file that includes:

- A list of funders that align with your mission, programs, and location.
- Notes on each funder's average grant size, deadlines, and application requirements.
- A top 10 list of funders to focus on.
- A better handle on how to review 990s using using Candid.
- Clear notes on which funders support capital, program, operating, or capacity-building grants.
- A simple folder or spreadsheet to organize your funder research (future-you will thank you).
- A "future prospects" list of funders to build relationships with, even if you're not applying yet.

LESSON 2 Key Takeaways

☑ *Start your funder search with trusted research tools (FDO, Candid, Instrumentl, GrantStation, Grant Gopher, Grants.gov, state/local government, libraries, banks, and community foundations).*

- ☑ *Match projects to funders based on mission alignment, not just availability.*
- ☑ *Build relationships early by following funders, attending webinars, and making personal connections.*
- ☑ *Tap into corporate funders, employee giving programs, and local businesses through your board, staff, volunteers, and donors.*
- ☑ *Use 990s to analyze giving history, average grant size, and funder priorities.*
- ☑ *Size your grant request strategically based on past giving data.*
- ☑ *Always check funder guidelines for geographic restrictions and giving ranges.*
- ☑ *Use AI tools to speed up funder research, analyze alignment, summarize 990s, and prioritize top prospects.*
- ☑ *Before applying, run a one-sentence alignment test: "This funder supports _____; we are requesting _____ to do _____."*

COMING UP NEXT Now that you've identified your needs and organized your research, it's time to set up simple systems to track everything and build a funder pipeline you can manage (without needing five extra staff). In *Lesson 3*, I will show you how to create **Your Grant Spreadsheet.**

Behind every successful grant is a story so compelling it leaves the funder no choice but to join your mission.

LESSON 3

Your Grant Spreadsheet: Organizing Your Grants Like a Pro

Now that you know what you need—and you've started identifying potential funders—it's time to get organized. Think of your **Grant Spreadsheet** as your control center: a central hub that keeps you grounded, focused, and ready for anything. It's where you track deadlines, contacts, submission statuses, and notes, so nothing slips through the cracks. It helps you spot opportunities, avoid surprises, and stay mission-focused without scrambling at the last minute.

NOTE *If your organization pays for software that allows you to track your grants, you may still find a few useful tips in this section. If not, feel free to move on to the next lesson.*

Why You Need a Grant Spreadsheet

This isn't just busy work. Your spreadsheet becomes your grant command center. It helps you:

- Track deadlines (no more "when was that due again?!").
- Prioritize which funders to focus on.
- Avoid missing details that could sink your proposal.

- Stay accountable when juggling multiple applications.
- Build institutional knowledge that your future self (and your whole team) will thank you for later.

What Goes into Your Spreadsheet

Here are your core "must-haves:"

Column	What to Track
Funder Name	The foundation, trust, or government agency
Website	Link to their website or grant application page
Contact Info	Name, email, phone – of a real person, if possible
Deadlines	LOI (letter of Inquiry) date, application date, report dates
Funding Priorities	What they like to fund: spay/neuter, education, capital, etc.
Geographic Focus	City, county, state, national
Typical Grant Size	Their usual giving range
Status	Researching, submitted, funded, declined, follow-up

A spreadsheet is only helpful if it's updated, so build good habits:

- Review your spreadsheet weekly.
- Remove funders who don't align with your mission/project.
- Update deadlines and contact information.
- Record feedback and funding decisions.
- Highlight strong renewal opportunities.

#29: Add a few extra columns for "Funder Fit," "Next Steps" and "Last Contacted"
These will save your sanity when you're tracking multiple funders over time.

#30: Your Grant Spreadsheet doesn't need to be fancy – it needs to be usable.
Excel, Google Sheets, Airtable – whatever you'll actually open regularly wins. It shouldn't live on a sticky note or in that mystery notebook you can never find when deadlines hit.

#19: Let AI help you analyze your organization's history.
Upload your past funded (and declined) grants into AI and ask: *"What patterns do you see in funder types, grant sizes, and success rates? Where should we prioritize reapplications?"* Sometimes your own history reveals exactly where you should double down—or where you may want to shift strategy.

LESSON 3   Key Takeaways

A strong spreadsheet doesn't just keep you organized—it helps you think like a strategist. It shows you where your best funding matches are, when to act, and how to track your progress over time. What starts as a simple tool quickly becomes your grant calendar, funder database, and proposal tracker—and eventually, your most valuable asset for building a sustainable funding pipeline.

It keeps your entire team aligned, focused, and pulling toward the same goals. And like a well-tended garden, the more thoughtfully you plant and care for it, the more it grows.

A grant spreadsheet should contain:

- ☑ *Columns tracking funder name, priorities, deadlines, contacts, and status.*
- ☑ *Notes on average grant sizes and geographic giving focus.*
- ☑ *A "Next Step" column so you always know your immediate task.*
- ☑ *Color codes or filters highlighting strongest funder matches.*
- ☑ *A system you'll review and update regularly (not just when deadlines loom).*
- ☑ *AI prompts to help you analyze your list, flag best fits, and work smarter.*

COMING UP NEXT Now that your needs are clear and your funder list is taking shape, it's time to focus on the writing itself. In *Lesson 4*, we'll work on your **Mission Statement** and **Your Organizational History**—two sections that pack a big punch.

Data proves the need, but stories move the heart — and great proposals need both.

LESSON 4

The Mission Statement and Your Organizational History: Highlighting Your History and Impact

Now that you've done the prep work, clarified your need, found good-fit funders, and organized your research, it's time to write.

But before you begin writing, remember this: grant writing isn't creative writing. It's structured, strategic communication.

Funders don't want poetic paragraphs or elaborate metaphors. They want clarity. They want alignment. They want to see that you understand their priorities and have a solid plan. Think like a journalist and a storyteller, backed by evidence, data, and mission-focus.

This chapter walks you through two of the most essential narrative elements funders almost always request: your **Mission Statement and Organizational History**. These are the foundations of your story and the building blocks for every proposal you write.

 **#31: *Keep it real, not promotional.***
If your proposal sounds like marketing copy, you're doing it wrong. Your copy should be persuasive, not gimmicky.

Your Mission Statement: The Compass for Everything

Your **Mission Statement** isn't just an opening line—it's the anchor of your proposal. Funders want to understand *who* you are and *why* you exist before they invest in *what* you do.

If you already have a mission statement, great—it likely came from your board and serves as the guiding compass for your organization. But if you're just getting started and don't have one yet, it's time to schedule a working session with your board. Be prepared to spend a day digging into your values, vision, and goals. It's often harder than it sounds to craft a statement that truly reflects everything you do.

A strong mission statement should:

- Clearly express your purpose, values, and goals.
- Highlight what makes your organization unique.
- Remind funders why your work matters—especially in the context of this grant.

#32: *Your mission is the throughline.*
Every part of your proposal should connect back to it. If something feels out of sync, don't ignore it—reframe it. When it comes to grants, alignment with your mission is essential.

Organizational History: Building Trust with Your Story

Once the funder knows what you're all about, they want to know where you've been. Your **Organizational History** gives context and credibility to your mission. But this is where many groups struggle. In all my years writing grants, this is the area where I see organizations get stuck. Simply put, many nonprofits don't keep track of their amazing history. I once worked with a group that tried to rebuild their history from old board notes, faded newsletters, newspaper microfilms, and one board member's memory of "the year with the flood." It was like putting together a jigsaw puzzle without the box top.

Don't wait until you need it. Build your history as you go. The sooner you start documenting impact year by year, the stronger your history becomes.

Funders typically want to know:

- When and why you were founded.
- Who you serve.
- Key milestones or growth over time.
- What makes your organization qualified to carry out this project.

But a strong organizational history is more than just a list of dates and services. It's a snapshot of your evolution. It's where you show your capacity, your credibility, and your character.

#33: Build your master history.
Write a full version of your history, and update it annually. Include a paragraph on every major program or service your organization offers. Tuck it into your digital grant folder, and pull sections as needed depending on the application.

#34: Mastering word–and character–count.
Sometimes, you'll have room to share your full story. Other times, you'll have just 500 characters—not words, characters—to make your case. It's like being asked to summarize your life's work on a Post-it note. Precision becomes your superpower. AI can help reduce your copy to a shorter version, but it can't always hit an exact character count (yet). Don't ask AI to work miracles. Instead, start by writing your best full version—then tighten from there.

Here's what a full organizational history might look like.

Compassion Pet Care Alliance Organizational History & Programs

Since its inception in 2012, Compassion Pet Care Alliance (CPCA) has been a beacon of hope for homeless and abandoned pets in our community. Founded by a group of dedicated animal lovers, CPCA began its journey by building a shelter with the capacity to house 200 pets—providing a safe haven for animals in need. With a mission to rescue and rehabilitate, CPCA quickly became a trusted resource for both pets and people.

In 2013, we launched our Spay/Neuter Program, aiming to reduce pet overpopulation and promote responsible ownership through low-cost surgeries. The following year, we expanded our reach with the Community Outreach and Education Program, offering workshops and presentations to empower individuals with knowledge about animal welfare.

In 2015, our Foster Care Network was established to provide temporary homes for animals requiring extra care or socialization, furthering our commitment to their well-being. The Seniors for Seniors Program, introduced in 2016, celebrated the bond between older pets and senior citizens, offering discounted adoption fees to encourage these meaningful connections.

As part of our ongoing efforts to serve the community, we launched the Animal-Assisted Therapy Program in 2017, bringing comfort and companionship to individuals facing various challenges. In 2018, we implemented a Trap-Neuter-Return (TNR) Program to manage community cat populations humanely, reflecting our dedication to sustainable solutions. The Humane Education Initiative, launched in 2019, engaged young people in learning experiences centered on empathy and compassion.

Despite the challenges posed by the COVID-19 pandemic in 2020, CPCA adapted its operations to continue serving animals in need. In 2021 and beyond, we have celebrated expansion and growth, increasing our facilities and programs to rescue, rehabilitate, and rehome even more pets.

Today, CPCA houses an average of 200 animals at a time, with thousands successfully adopted into loving homes. Through every initiative, we remain steadfast in our mission to create a more humane world for all creatures.

#20: Need a tighter version of your organization's history?

I entered the full copy into AI and used this prompt: "Tighten this to one paragraph." Here's what AI produced:

Since its inception in 2012, Compassion Pet Care Alliance (CPCA) has been a beacon of hope for homeless and abandoned pets in our community. Founded by a group of dedicated animal lovers, CPCA began by building a shelter with the capacity to house 200 pets, creating a safe haven for animals in need. Over the years, we launched programs to address every stage of animal welfare: a Spay/Neuter Program to reduce overpopulation (2013), a Community Outreach and Education to empower pet owners (2014), a Foster Care Network for animals needing extra care (2015), and the Seniors for Seniors Program to connect older pets with senior citizens (2016). We expanded further with an Animal-Assisted Therapy Program (2017), a Trap-Neuter-Return initiative for feral cats (2018), and a Humane Education Initiative to engage young people (2019). Even during the COVID-19 pandemic, CPCA adapted and continued to serve, and today we house an average of 200 animals at a time while facilitating thousands of adoptions. Through every program, CPCA has remained steadfast in its mission to rescue, rehabilitate, and rehome pets while creating a more humane community for all.

LESSON 4 Key Takeaways

☑ Before you dive into **Goals**, **Objectives**, and **Timelines**, make sure your **Mission** and **Organization History** are strong, clear, and aligned.

☑ Your **Mission** shows the funder who you are and why your work matters. This is the board-approved statement that guides all of your work.

☑ Your **Organizational History** shows you have the experience and credibility to succeed. This should include how you got started and your evolution through the years.

COMING UP NEXT Now that you've captured your **Mission** and **History**, *Lesson 5* explains how to write one of the most important parts of your grant proposal: the **Needs Statement**.

A good budget shows what you need. A great budget shows you've thought through every step to get there.

LESSON 5

The Needs (or Problem) Statement: Building a Case for Why This Work Matters

If your grant proposal were a house, the **Needs Statement** would be the foundation. It's where you establish the problem your program is built to solve—and why it matters right now. Without a solid foundation, the rest of the proposal can't stand. This is your chance to show funders exactly why your program exists, who is affected, and why their support is urgently needed.

Funders don't always label it as a **Needs Statement**, though. Sometimes they call it "**Problem Statement**," "**Statement of Need**, or just "**Background**." If they don't ask for a **Needs Statement**, then roll it into your **Project Narrative** (*Lesson 6*). No matter where it lives, every strong proposal has a clear explanation of why your work is necessary and why their funding matters.

Too often, people confuse a **Needs Statement** with simply describing what their organization does:

"We provide low-cost spay/neuter services." That statement is a fact about one of your programs, but it doesn't explain your need.

Your **Needs Statement** should answer the following questions:

* *What problem are you trying to solve?*
* *Who is impacted?*
* *Why does this problem matter?*
* *Why now?*
* *What will happen if nothing is done?*

Imagine a shelter overflowing with kittens during Spring. You don't just say:

"We're full of kittens in the Spring."

You "show" them the situation through your description of what is happening: *"Each spring, our shelter sees a 300% increase in stray kittens as unsterilized community cats give birth. Without intervention, many of these kittens' face euthanasia or die in the wild from illness, injury, or starvation. In [YEAR], 1,842 kittens entered our shelter—more than double our capacity."*

Now the funder can see the urgency, scale, and stakes.

#35: *Show the need, loud and clear.*

No matter what the funder calls it, your job is always the same: Show the need clearly, specifically, and urgently. Don't assume funders automatically understand the challenges animals and pet owners face in your community—spell it out for them.

Avoid General Statements

Weak: *"There are too many unaltered pets in the community."*

Stronger: *"In the three ZIP codes we serve, 68% of owned pets remain unaltered due to cost, transportation barriers, and limited clinic availability. These areas also show a 19% increase in owner surrenders of pets, compared with the rest of the city.*

#36: *Use local data whenever possible.*

Funders want to see that you know your community, not just the national picture. Local statistics show that your program is grounded in the real needs of the people and animals you serve.

The Three Parts of a "Needs Statement"

1. The Problem: Describe the issue clearly. Use real numbers, local data, and concrete examples.

"Veterinary deserts leave more than 5,000 pets in our service area without access to affordable care."

2. Who is Impacted: Show who is affected—animals, people, neighborhoods.

"Low-income pet owners often delay care due to cost, risking preventable illnesses like parvo, distemper, and upper respiratory disease."

3. Why It Matters: Explain the consequences of inaction and the urgency to act.

"Without intervention, sick and unvaccinated pets increase shelter intake, disease outbreaks, and public safety concerns."

#37: *Show funders what you see every day.*

Never assume funders understand your world. Paint the full picture, but stay focused. You don't need 10 pages of statistics. A tight two to three paragraphs with the right data and real-world examples will do more heavy lifting than pages of filler.

A Sample Needs Statement Paragraph

In our city's underserved neighborhoods, cost and transportation prevent thousands of families from accessing basic veterinary care. In 2023, our shelter saw a 17% increase in owner surrenders directly tied to untreated medical conditions. Left unaddressed, these gaps drive up shelter intake, strain city resources, and leave animals at greater risk of euthanasia. Our program provides free preventive care directly in these communities to keep pets healthy, safe, and in their homes.

#21: *Use AI to strengthen your Needs Statement.*

Paste your rough draft into AI and ask: *"Help me strengthen this needs statement for a grant proposal. Does it clearly show the problem, who's impacted, and why it matters?"* Remember to feed AI your program data to help fine-tune the language, otherwise, AI might make things up.

LESSON 5 Key Takeaways

- ☑ The **Needs Statement** is the foundation your grant proposal stands on.
- ☑ Always explain why your program exists and why funding is needed right now.
- ☑ Funders may call it a **"Needs Statement"**, "problem statement," "background," or something else—but the core purpose is always the same.
- ☑ Don't confuse your services with your need; describe the problem, not just what you do.
- ☑ Answer five key questions: What is the problem? Who is impacted? Why does it matter? Why now? What happens if nothing is done?
- ☑ Use clear data, real numbers, and local examples to bring urgency and scale.
- ☑ Avoid vague or general statements—be specific and focused.
- ☑ A strong needs statement includes: The problem, who is impacted, and why it matters.
- ☑ Keep it clear, brief (two to three strong paragraphs), and focused on your community.
- ☑ Use AI to review, strengthen, and fine-tune your **Needs Statement** draft.

COMING UP NEXT In *Lesson 6*, we'll break down how to write your **Project Narrative**—where you show funders exactly *what* you plan to do, *how* you'll do it, and *who* you'll serve. This is where your **Needs Statement** turns into a clear plan of action.

LESSON 6

The Project Narrative: Turning Your Mission into Action

Now that you've introduced your organization, it's time to build the heart of your proposal—the **Project Narrative** (sometimes called the Project Description, Program Narrative or Program Description). This is where your grant moves from *"here's who we are"* to *"here's exactly how we're going to put your money to work."*

This is the framework that supports everything else. It gives your ideas structure, shows how each part connects, and proves the foundation is solid. Without it, the rest of the proposal—your goals, budget, evaluation—has nowhere to stand. A strong narrative doesn't just describe what you'll do. It invites the funder to walk through the project with you, step-by-step, to see the impact their investment will make in the community. This section should feel *logical, thorough, and actionable.*

At its core, this section answers six key questions—what journalists call the *"5 W's and 1 H Framework."* This classic journalistic and communications tool helps ensure your project or program is clearly and completely described. Whether you're writing a grant, a news story, or a program summary, answering these **Core Six** questions, (which is how I will refer to them going forward), gives your reader all the essential information they need to understand the project.

- **Who**—Who is involved? Describe the people, partners, or populations involved. This might include your staff, collaborators, or the community you're serving.

- **What**—What is the program or service? Explain what you're doing—your core service, event, intervention, or activity.

- **Where**—Where will it happen? Give the location(s), neighborhoods, or platforms where the work will take place.

- **When**—When will it take place? Provide the timing or schedule: start/end dates, frequency, or seasonality.

- **Why**—Why is this needed? Define the problem you're addressing and explain why your approach matters. This is your case for support.

- **How**—How will it be carried out? This is the **Implementation Plan** (*Lesson 10*). Describe the step-by-step process, tools, staffing, and methods used to deliver the work.

#38: *The Core Six questions.*
The **Core Six** questions connect the dots between the problem you're solving and the solution you're offering. This is your blueprint—and your best opportunity to show the funder you've done your homework, and that your team is ready to deliver results.

Funders are looking for alignment with their priorities, not abstract ideas or vague good intentions. Let's look at a sample **Project Narrative** for vaccine clinics with annotations on what each section answers for the funder, so you can see exactly how the Core Six plays out in real-world grant writing.

Sample Project Narrative

Closing the Care Gap: Free Pet Vaccinations in Underserved Communities

A recent client, Sarah, found a stray dog and felt compelled to care for him despite her financial constraints. Thankfully, by attending one of our vaccine clinics, she gained access to affordable pet care, ensuring her new furry companion received essential vaccinations and microchipping. At the same time, we scheduled Sarah's new dog for his neuter surgery. This support not only benefited Sarah and her dog but also contributed to our mission of bridging the gap in access to care for pets in underserved communities, ultimately reducing owner surrenders of pets, unwanted litters, and homeless pets roaming the streets.

▶ *This opening story gives a human face to the problem ("Who" and "Why"). It emotionally engages the reader and shows the real-life challenge you're solving.*

Every day, we encounter people like Sarah who face barriers to providing proper care for their pets, often due to financial limitations, a lack of veterinary care in the neighborhood, and no reliable transportation to reach clinics located miles away.

▶ *Further reinforces the "Why" — the root problem you're solving.*

Many of the neighborhoods we serve are classified as "veterinary deserts"—areas with limited or no access to affordable veterinary services within 10 to 15 miles. These communities also face compounding public safety and shelter challenges. In 20XX alone, animal control logged over 3,200 stray animal calls from just five ZIP codes, accounting for 42% of all citywide reports. Dog bites in these same neighborhoods occur at rates 2.5 times higher than the city average, and 58% of shelter intakes from these areas involve litters born to unsterilized pets.

▶ *This data grounds your argument, providing clear evidence of need. Funder box checked.*

To address these challenges directly where they occur, we bring free vaccine clinics into underserved neighborhoods. These mobile events eliminate transportation barriers and ensure that pets receive essential core vaccines, microchips, and access to spay/neuter scheduling all in one visit.

▶ *What you're doing (What), for whom (Who), and Where and When.*

We seek funding to support 10 free vaccine clinics in 15 underserved neighborhoods—identified through poverty rates, limited veterinary access, high reports of dog bites, stray animals, and owner surrenders to the city shelter, totaling $50,000 in annual operating costs. Each clinic costs approximately $5,000 to staff, transport, and supply with vaccines and microchips for 100 dogs and cats. These clinics will be held over a 12-month period.

▶ *What you're asking for (Amount / Budget clarity). This also shows the "How."*

In addition to preventing disease, these clinics allow us to educate pet owners about responsible pet care and schedule sterilization surgeries that prevent unwanted litters, reducing future shelter intake. They also help ensure that pets who may enter the shelter system later are already vaccinated, lowering the risk of disease outbreaks that could shut down shelter operations.

▶ *Long-term impact — "Why" this matters now and down the road.*

Program success will be measured through clinic records, tracking the number of pets vaccinated and scheduled for surgery, as well as ZIP code-based shelter data on intake and disease outbreaks. We will compare year-over-year metrics to assess reductions in surrenders and improvements in shelter intake in targeted areas.

▶ *Evaluation criteria added — answering "How will you know it worked?"*

We are requesting a $10,000 grant from the You Are So Kind Foundation to cover the costs of two of these 10 vaccine clinics in 20XX.

▶ *Specific ask: clear, concrete, time-bound request ("When") — example of funding.*

Breaking Down the Building Blocks

You've anchored your proposal in both story (Sarah) and data (animal control stats) — a powerful one-two punch that connects emotionally while grounding your ask, (see *Lesson 8: Stories and Data: Crafting Proposals That Connect and Convince*).

Here's why this approach builds funder confidence:

- It covers all the Core Six: Who, What, Where, When, Why, and How.
- It includes clear, compelling numbers.
- It shows you're strategic, prepared, and aligned with funder priorities.

You've also included the essential building blocks of a strong proposal — all of which are covered in this book:

- **The Story** — Sarah's experience gives your proposal a human face *(Lesson 8)*.
- **The Need** — Underserved neighborhoods, poverty, vet deserts, strays, dog bites, and shelter surrenders *(Lesson 5)*.
- **The Solution** — Free vaccine clinics — 10 total, reaching 100 pets per clinic *(Lesson 6)*.
- **The Budget** — Request amount and cost per clinic clearly outlined *(Lesson 1)*.
- **The Implementation and Timeline** — Staffing, transportation, supplies, and scheduling are clearly defined *(Lesson 10)*.
- **The Impact** — The impact of this proposal goes far beyond reducing shelter disease. By providing free clinics in underserved areas, it increases access to preventive care, helps reduce owner surrenders and unwanted litters, and improves public safety in neighborhoods with high stray and dog bite rates. It also strengthens community trust by meeting people where they are and offering real solutions that keep pets healthy and at home. *(Lesson 11)*.

#39: *Be crystal clear.*
When you write, you have to assume your funder has never toured your shelter, visited your clinic, or walked your neighborhoods. Your job is to paint the picture so vividly they won't need Google Maps to understand your work, your clients, or your impact.

7 Ways to Make Your Narrative Even Better

While this is a solid narrative that checks all the major boxes, here are seven enhancements that can take your proposal from "good" to "highly fundable." These elements show depth, foresight, and alignment with what many funders are looking for.

1 Community Partnerships

Example: *We partner with local animal control officers, community health departments, neighborhood associations, and school-based outreach programs to help identify clinic sites, promote events, and increase participation among pet owners most in need.*

▶ *This adds credibility, shows collaboration, and demonstrates broad community support for the program. Funders love to see you're not working in a vacuum.*

2 Sustainability / Long-Term Vision

Example: *This grant will not only fund two vaccine clinics in 2024, but also serve as a model for expanding the program to additional neighborhoods through future partnerships, in-kind donations, and community engagement.*

▶ *Funders love to see this. It shows you're thinking long-term and building momentum — not just filling a short-term gap.*

3 Staff & Volunteer Expertise

Example: *Our medical team includes licensed veterinarians and trained technicians who deliver high-quality care during each clinic. Bilingual volunteers assist with client intake, education, and scheduling follow-up spay/neuter surgeries.*

▶ *Reinforces your organization's ability to complete the project. Helps funders feel confident their money is in experienced, qualified hands.*

④ Client Education Component (Small but Powerful)

Example: *Each clinic also includes brief client education on responsible pet care, the importance of sterilization, and how to access low-cost veterinary resources year-round.*

▶ *Adds value for the funder. Shows you're not just offering a one-time service—you're building long-term impact by educating and empowering pet owners.*

⑤ Equity & Access Statement

Example: *By bringing services directly into these neighborhoods, we reduce transportation, language, and financial barriers that too often prevent pet owners from accessing care for their animals.*

▶ *Many funders actively look for this. Demonstrating a commitment to equity shows you're aware of systemic barriers and working intentionally to overcome them.*

⑥ Clear "How" (Implementation Plan)

Example: *Clinics will be held monthly in rotating ZIP codes. Outreach staff will schedule events, coordinate volunteers, and track outcomes. Services will be delivered through our mobile unit and supported by bilingual educators.*

▶ *Describes how the work will happen. Funders want more than vision—they want to know your plan is realistic, actionable, and well-organized.*

⑦ Evaluation & Outcomes

Example: *We will track the number of pets vaccinated, spay/neuter appointments scheduled, and ZIP codes served. We'll also collect participant feedback to assess impact and improve services.*

▶ *Shows you're measuring success, not just hoping for it. Funders want to see data and a feedback loop—not just activity.*

#40: *Avoid vague language.*
Don't assume the funder understands your community or service model. Skip the buzzwords and get specific. Funders don't fund *"awareness."* They fund *"action."*

#41: *The more specific you are, the stronger your narrative becomes.*
You want the funder to say: *"Ah—I can clearly see where my money is going."*

#22: *Writer's Block. Let AI get you started.*
AI can help you turn your bullet points into a starting paragraph when you feel stuck staring at that blank screen. AI can even help you convert a rough outline into a clean draft. Just remember: YOU bring the knowledge. AI helps shape it.

BOOT CAMP SIDEBAR
6 Tips for All-Volunteer Organizations

If you're a small or all-volunteer group, this is often where the anxiety kicks in: *"Will funders take us seriously without paid staff?"*

The honest answer? Sometimes, they hesitate. Funders know that when people are paid, they're more likely to stay. Volunteers can walk away at any time. This makes funders think: *"If I give you money and your leadership changes next year, what happens to my grant?"*

That's the worry, and to be honest it can be a hurdle. but that doesn't mean you can't secure funding. Your job is to address those concerns head-on: show stability, leadership strength, and your ability to deliver. Here's how to make your case.

❶ Emphasize Stability in Leadership

Funders want confidence that your leadership won't disappear next year.

- Share how long your board or core leadership team has been in place.
- Appoint a volunteer Executive Director or Program Lead (even unpaid) to show structure.
- If possible, seek funding for a part-time grant funded position to reassure funders.

Example: *An all-volunteer community cat group has operated under the same leader for 20 years. Despite no paid staff, their leadership stability gives funders confidence.*

❷ Highlight Cost-Effectiveness

Your volunteer model means nearly every dollar goes directly to animals, not overhead—and funders like knowing their money has real impact. Include data showing the percentage of your budget spent on programs vs. administration.

- Say it clearly: *"95% of every dollar directly supports veterinary care, adoption, and community outreach."*
- Remind funders that your low overhead allows limited dollars to stretch further.

3. Showcase Professional Strengths of Your Volunteer Team

You may not have paid staff, but you likely have serious expertise sitting at your leadership table.

- *"Our board includes a CPA, a retired veterinarian, an attorney, a local food bank director, and a corporate HR executive."*
- These professional skill sets provide financial oversight, legal compliance, and management capability—without payroll costs.
- Call out any board fundraising experience, nonprofit leadership, or prior grant experience as well.

4. Leverage Your Foster-Based Model (If Applicable)

Foster-based programs, a system where homeless, abandoned, or at-risk animals are placed into temporary, home-based care instead of, or in addition to, a traditional shelter environment, offer individualized care while minimizing costs.

- Highlight foster retention rates, adoption success stories, and the cost savings compared to a brick-and-mortar shelter model.
- Share how this model helps reduce euthanasia, improve animal outcomes, and build community engagement.

5. Demonstrate Strong Governance & Infrastructure

Funders want to know your organization is stable and accountable, even without paid staff.

- Describe your board's role in oversight, strategic planning, and financial management.
- Mention written policies for financial controls, record-keeping, and operations.
- Show you have systems in place to track outcomes, monitor finances, and deliver grant reports on time.

6. Show Your Track Record

Funders fund results—show them yours.

- Share your adoption numbers, spay/neuter surgeries, TNR efforts, volunteer service hours, or community education programs.
- If you've previously received grant funding or community support, name prior funders or partnerships.
- Show how you've grown your impact over time.

You're not apologizing for being an all-volunteer organization. You're positioning it as a strength. Funders care about stability, ability, and results. If you proactively address their concerns and you can show what your organization is capable of, your all-volunteer model can make you a very attractive investment.

What if They Ask for an "Executive Summary"?

Most funders won't ask for an **Executive Summary**, but occasionally one will. When they do, they are simply asking you for a clear, fast snapshot of your full proposal—something they can grasp in 30 seconds to help them decide whether to read the rest.

Although it may appear first in the grant application, always write it last after you've completed your full proposal. That way, you're pulling from your strongest content, not guessing at the beginning.

Your **Executive Summary** should be tight, compelling, and hit the essentials:

- A brief overview of the problem you're solving and your proposed solution.
- Who will benefit from the funding.
- The program goals and outcomes you're targeting.
- Your total project budget and amount requested.
- A strong closing call to action—what you're asking for and why now is the right time to fund this.

Here is a sample of what the previous **Project Narrative** might look like as an executive summary.

Closing the Care Gap – Free Pet Vaccinations in Underserved Communities

In underserved neighborhoods across our city, thousands of pets face preventable illness, pet owners struggle to access affordable care, and shelters continue to see high intake of unsterilized animals. Many of these communities are classified as "veterinary deserts," with no affordable veterinary services available within 10 to 15 miles. In 20XX alone, animal control responded to over 3,200 stray animal calls from just five ZIP codes, representing 42% of all citywide reports. Dog bites in these same neighborhoods occur at rates 2.5 times higher than the city average, and 58% of shelter intakes involve litters born to unsterilized pets.

▶ ***Problem Statement:** This quickly explains why this work matters. It uses specific, relevant data to ground the funder in the urgency of the issue.*

To address these challenges, we operate mobile vaccine clinics directly in the neighborhoods most affected. These free clinics eliminate transportation and financial barriers by providing core vaccines, microchips, and access to spay/neuter scheduling all in one visit—protecting both public and animal health, while reducing future shelter intake. In addition, each clinic serves as an opportunity for client education on responsible pet care and sterilization benefits.

▶ ***Solution Summary:** This clearly outlines what you're doing, who you're helping, where, and why it's effective—all in a few sentences.*

We are requesting a $10,000 grant from the You Are So Kind Foundation *to fund two free vaccine clinics in 2024. This is part of a larger program to operate 10 clinics in 5 underserved neighborhoods over the next year, serving approximately 1,000 pets while reducing unwanted litters, preventing disease outbreaks, and easing pressure on our city shelter system.*

▶ **Funding Request:** *This delivers the "ask"—how much is needed, for what specific activity, and the impact it will create.*

#42: Don't overthink the executive summary.
This isn't where you introduce new information—it's where you reinforce the strongest points from your full proposal. You're simply giving the funder a "preview of coming attractions." Once your full narrative is written, pulling this summary together becomes surprisingly easy.

#23: Unsure where to start your executive summary?
Paste your full **Project Narrative** into AI and say: *"Summarize this into a 1 to 2 paragraph executive summary for a grant funder. Focus on the problem, solution, who benefits, and the funding request."*

AI can help you distill your content into a funder-friendly format while you fine-tune the language.

LESSON 6 Key Takeaways

☑ You've built a full **Project Narrative** using the Core Six Questions (Who, What, When, Where, Why and How).

☑ You've written a clear, funder-centered project description that avoids vague language and focuses on action.

☑ You've connected your work to real community needs, backed by both stories and data.

☑ You've created a simple executive summary to help funders quickly understand your request.

COMING UP NEXT Now that you've built your **Project Narrative**, we'll take a deeper dive in *Lesson 7* on how to write your **Goals and Objectives**, including what the difference is, what funders really want to know, and how to write them both like a pro.

LESSON 7

Goals and Objectives: Showing Funders You Will Get Results

You've developed your **Project Narrative**—what you do, why it matters, and who you help. Now it's time to answer the question every funder wants to know:

"If we fund you, how will we know it's working?"

Funders aren't just investing in passion. They're investing in progress. They have a board of directors to answer to, impact reports to deliver, and limited dollars to spend—so they need to feel confident that your program will deliver real results.

That's where your **Goals and Objectives** come in. When done right, they:

- Build funder confidence in your ability to deliver.
- Show them that you're focused on outcomes, not just effort.
- Make reporting ten times easier down the road.

But before you can write, you need to know the difference between a **Goal** and an **Objective** – and why both matter to the funder.

You can't map a route if you don't know where you're going. That's why you always start with your Goal—the "why" behind your work.

GOALS = The Big Picture

What are you ultimately trying to achieve? Think broad impact.

Now you are ready to write your objectives. These are the actionable, time-bound benchmarks that show how you plan to make your Goal happen.

OBJECTIVES = The Measurable Steps

Your Objectives should answer the "how," "when," and "how much." Here are some examples.

Example:
Goal: Reduce pet overpopulation in underserved communities.
Objective: Spay/neuter 1,000 cats and dogs in 10 targeted ZIP codes by December 31.

Pretty straightforward, right? That's the point. A strong **Goal** paired with a clear, measurable **Objective** tells the funder exactly what you plan to do, and should be easy for them to understand. You should always be able to explain your project in just a few sentences, and with character counts and word limits on some applications, you may have no choice but to do just that.

 **#43:** *If your Objective starts with "We want to help...,"* Try reframing it with a number, a deadline, and an action verb.

Sometimes, **Goals** are written too vaguely—and that can weaken your entire proposal. Let's look at a few examples.

Goals: Weak vs. Strong

Weak (too vague):
- "We want to help animals."
- "We want to improve access to care."

Strong (clear & funder-friendly):
- "We want to improve pet health and reduce shelter intake by expanding access to affordable preventive care (vaccines, microchips, and spay/neuter) for up to 300 dogs and cats in underserved neighborhoods."

The takeaway? Start with the big picture. Strong goals give funders clarity and confidence. Your objectives are simply proof you can follow through with what you want to do.

BOOT CAMP SIDEBAR
Tips for Writing a Strong Goal

❶ Connect your goal to the bigger picture

Don't just say what you'll do. Say why it matters.

Weak: *"We want to launch a new clinic."*

Stronger: *"We want to increase access to preventive care in underserved communities by launching a new low-cost veterinary clinic."*

❷ Keep it big-picture but grounded in your mission.

A goal should feel ambitious but still rooted in what your organization actually does. The goal is the destination, not the step-by-step directions.

❸ Link your goal to community impact.

Funders care about animals and the people who love them. The strongest goals make that connection.

Example: *"To reduce shelter intake and improve pet health outcomes in low-income neighborhoods by expanding access to affordable veterinary care."*

❹ Avoid jargon or internal language.

Words like *"enhance programming"* or *"build capacity"* are vague. Say what you really mean—in plain English.

Weak: *"We aim to enhance programming and build capacity in underserved communities."*

Strong: *"We plan to offer 10 monthly pet wellness clinics in targeted ZIP codes and train five new volunteers to expand these services and reach more pet parents in underserved neighborhoods."*

❺ Align it with the funder's priorities.

Strong goals often mirror the language and values of the funder. If they focus on equity, prevention, or access to care, your goal should too.

Example: *"To increase equitable access to basic veterinary care in high-need neighborhoods through mobile clinics that eliminate cost and transportation barriers."*

#44: One clear sentence = one clear goal.
If your goal can't fit into one clear sentence, you haven't simplified it enough yet.

#45: Objectives should fit the goal—and prove it.
If your objectives don't roll up into a clear goal—or your goal doesn't have any trackable objectives—you're not ready to write that grant yet.

#46: When funders ask for "common goals," they're looking for shared purpose—how your work connects to their mission.
This is different from simply stating your organization's goals or your project's goals. It's about showing how your work helps the funder achieve the outcomes they care about. The stronger the alignment, the stronger your proposal.

Writing SMART Objectives

Once your **Goal** is set, now it's time to build your **Objectives**. These are your guideposts for success. They show the funder how you'll turn your big-picture vision into measurable results.

To get it right, make sure your objectives are **SMART**—**S**pecific, **M**easurable, **A**chievable, **R**elevant, and **T**ime-bound—so funders can see exactly what you plan to do, how you'll do it, and when.

S – Specific

Say exactly *what* you're going to do. Avoid vague language like "raise awareness" or "help more animals." Be clear and concrete.

Instead of: *"Improve access to veterinary care"*

Try: *"Improve access to veterinary care by providing free vaccinations for 500 pets in five underserved ZIP codes."*

M – Measurable

How will you track it? If you can't count it, track it, or report it, it's not measurable. Funders want proof—not potential.

A – Achievable

Is it realistic? Set a goal you can realistically accomplish with the time, staff, and resources you have. Big dreams are great, just don't overpromise. Don't say you'll spay/neuter every cat in the ZIP code if you only have one vet on staff.

R – Relevant

Does your project align with their funding priorities? Make sure your **Goals and Objectives** align with your mission and the funder's guidelines. If the funder is focused on equity or underserved communities, your objective should reflect that as well.

T – Time-bound

When will it happen? Add a deadline. Funders want to know *when* this will happen, not just that it will happen "someday."

Instead of: *"Launch a pilot program to support pet owners"*

Try: *"Launch a 6-month pilot program by March 1 to provide free pet food to 300 families living in underserved neighborhoods."*

The clearer you are, the easier it is for funders to say "yes", so take your time, get specific, and show them exactly what success will look like.

#47: *Don't overload your proposal with too many Objectives.*
Pick 2 to 4 solid SMART objectives that clearly show how you'll move the needle. Remember: Goals inspire. Objectives prove.

Weak vs. Strong Objectives

Let's compare some weak and strong objectives, so you can see the difference more clearly.

Weak (Don't do this):

- We will raise awareness about pet wellness.
- We plan to support local pet owners.
- We will help reduce intake at the city shelter by microchipping dogs and cats.

Strong (This is what funders want):

- We will host three community vaccine clinics offering free rabies and parvo/distemper shots for 250 dogs and cats, total.
- Going door-to-door, we will distribute 5,000 flyers in four targeted ZIP codes.
- We will train and onboard 25 new volunteers to support weekend adoption events.
- We will recruit 100 new foster caregivers by December [YEAR].

- We will host 12 free vaccine clinics for 1,200 pets (100 each clinic) in underserved areas.
- We will increase return-to-owner rates by 20% in five ZIP codes by microchipping 500 dogs and cats.

#48: *Write SMART objectives for your project goal.*
Keep them SMART—Specific, Measurable, Achievable, Relevant, and Time-bound.

#24: *Struggling with vague goals?*
Ask AI to reframe your objective into a SMART Objective. But remember, you have to feed AI the information, including the stats you want to use, before it can produce anything meaningful you can use.

Example Program Objectives

Let's take a look at a Mobile Vaccine Clinic Project. This example includes four distinct goals, each with a set of SMART objectives. You don't have to include this many in your actual proposal—but seeing how a single program can have multiple layers of impact can help you identify what your program is really achieving.

▶ *Think of this like a brainstorming tool. Start broad to capture all the ways your program helps. Then, narrow it down and align with the funder's priorities. Every Objective here answers the one question funders are always asking: "If I give you money, what will change?"*

GOAL 1 Expand Access to Veterinary Care

We will host 10 free vaccine clinics in underserved neighborhoods by December 31, 20XX, reaching at least 1,000 pets (about 100 per clinic).

SMART Objectives:
- **Specific:** 10 clinics, 1,000 pets in target areas.
- **Measurable:** Clinic count and pet tally.
- **Achievable:** Matches outreach capacity.
- **Relevant:** Addresses veterinary care access gaps.

- **Time-bound:** Completion by December 31, 20XX.

▶ *Why + Who: Defining your access-to-care gap and the pet owners in veterinary deserts who are underserved.*

GOAL 2 Reduce Shelter Intake & Owner Surrenders

By December 31, 20XX, we will reduce owner surrenders from target ZIP codes by 20%, as measured by city shelter intake data, through preventive care and community outreach.

SMART Objectives:
- **Specific:** 20% drop in owner surrenders.
- **Measurable:** Verified via intake reports.
- **Achievable:** Based on historical patterns.
- **Relevant:** Direct tie to prevention strategy.
- **Time-bound:** Measured by year-end.

▶ *Why + Who: Identifying patterns of surrender and helping struggling pet owners keep their pets at home.*

GOAL 3 Eliminate Transportation Barriers

All 10 clinics will be hosted within communities lacking access to veterinary care, based on distance-to-clinic mapping and Census transportation data.

SMART Objectives:
- **Specific:** 100% of events in underserved ZIPs.
- **Measurable:** Tracked via mapping and ZIP code analysis.
- **Achievable:** Matches outreach design.
- **Relevant:** Tackles critical access barrier.
- **Time-bound:** Scheduled by December 31, 20XX.

▶ *Why + Who: Reaching people who can't access care due to lack of transportation, income, or nearby clinics.*

GOAL 4 Reduce Shelter Disease Risk

By year-end, we will vaccinate at least 1,000 pets prior to potential shelter intake, aiming to reduce shelter disease outbreaks by 10%.

SMART Objectives:
- **Specific:** 1,000 vaccinations; 10% disease reduction.
- **Measurable:** Tracked via clinic data and shelter medical reports.
- **Achievable:** Fits clinic capabilities.

- **Relevant:** Reduces risk for entire shelter system.
- **Time-bound:** All by December 31, 20XX.

▶ *Why + Who: Preventing disease by vaccinating pets before they ever reach the shelter door.*

Condensing for a Proposal

You wouldn't include all this detail in most grant applications. But understanding the full scope helps you write with clarity, purpose, and strategy. Once you've outlined the full range of impact, you can condense it like this:

Sample Condensed Version for a Grant

Goal: Increase access to preventive veterinary care in underserved communities.

Objectives:

- Host 10 mobile vaccine clinics by December 31, 20XX.
- Provide core vaccinations to 1,000 pets in target ZIP codes.
- Reduce owner surrenders from these areas by 20%.
- Improve shelter health outcomes by reducing disease-related intake by 10%.

#49: *Start big to see all the angles—then edit down.*
Funders don't need everything. They just need to know what you'll do, why it matters, and how success will be measured.

#25: *Ask AI to condense your long-form Goals and Objectives into a grant ready summary.*
"Condense these goals and objectives into a short summary that fits a grant application." Use the AI draft as a starting point, then revise to sound like your organization.

What to Do When Asking for General Operating Support

General operating support may be unrestricted, but it's not a blank check. Funders still want to know: *What will this investment allow you to accomplish?*

Even if you're not applying for a specific project, you're not off the hook. You still need to show that your organization delivers measurable value—and that continued funding will help you sustain or grow that impact.

When writing a general operating grant, focus on:

- **Your core services, who they support, and the people they reach** — spay/neuter, adoptions, community outreach, etc.
- **Your consistent outcomes** — the numbers you can reliably report every year.
- **Your long-term goals** — how general support moves you closer to your mission.
- **Why unrestricted support matters** — flexibility often equals stability, efficiency, and growth.

Example:

Goal: *Sustain core spay/neuter, vaccine, and adoption programs that serve 5,000 animals annually.*

Objective: *Perform 2,500 spay/neuter surgeries, provide 3,000 free or low-cost vaccinations, and place 1,000 animals into adoptive homes in 2025.*

#50: *Always write two to three SMART objectives funders can measure, even for general support.*
Tie them back to the funder's priorities when possible. Keep a few polished versions on hand in your digital grant folder for future use.

LESSON 7 Key Takeaways

- ☑ *Funders don't expect perfection, but they do expect a clear plan.*

- ☑ *Strong proposals include both **Goals** (your big-picture mission) and **Objectives** (specific, measurable actions you'll take). Your **Goals** answer: What are you trying to accomplish? Your **Objectives** answer: How will you accomplish it? How much? By when?*

- ☑ *Use **SMART Objectives** to show funders exactly what success looks like. Measurable objectives build funder confidence because they show you know how to track progress.*

- ☑ *Even if you don't hit 100% of your targets, funders appreciate organizations that are working toward achieving **Goals**.*

COMING UP NEXT In *Lesson 8*, we'll tackle how to make your proposal unforgettable — by using **Stories and Data** to bring your work to life.

When you show funders exactly how you'll measure success, you're also showing them you're worth betting on.

LESSON 8

Stories and Data: Crafting Proposals That Connect and Convince

Stories and **Data** serve two essential roles in a grant proposal—think of them as the left brain and right brain working together. **Stories** spark emotion, paint vivid pictures, and bring your mission to life. They help funders connect with the people and animals you serve. **Data**, on the other hand, appeals to logic. It offers measurable proof, demonstrates credibility, and shows that your programs are effective and worthy of investment. A strong proposal benefits from both: stories to engage, data to validate. Together, they create a balanced, funder-ready proposal that speaks to both heart and mind.

Why Stories Matter

If you've ever felt unsure about whether to include **Stories** in your proposal, let me settle it right now: stories belong. In fact, they're one of your most powerful tools.

You can have the strongest **Data**, the most carefully written **Objectives**, and the clearest budget—but without **Stories**, your proposal risks feeling flat. **Stories** create the emotional doorway that invites funders to care. They help funders not only understand your work but feel why it matters.

Stories humanize your work. They put a face to your mission. They turn a need into something personal and urgent.

Funders may have policies to follow and boards to answer to, but at the end of the day, they're still people. They care. And while they may fund programs based on alignment and capacity, their decision is often influenced by something deeper: connection. A good story taps into that connection. It reminds them why your work matters—in the real world, to real people, with real stakes.

For example, you could tell a funder: *"We need funding to launch a transport program in underserved neighborhoods."*

That's accurate. But it doesn't breathe.

Or you could say: *"Last month, an 83-year-old woman walked a mile with her dog in a wagon to get him neutered—without complaint, without fanfare—simply trying to do the right thing for her pet."*

That story makes your need visible. It creates urgency, empathy, and impact—all in just a few sentences. **Stories** aren't just emotional hooks; they're the why behind the what.

Here's how you can tell a story without naming a specific individual—by painting a vivid picture of the community need instead:

In Texas, 68% of fatal dog bite victims are children under the age of 12—a sobering statistic that underscores the urgent need for early education around pet care, compassion, and dog safety. In Fort Worth, this issue is even more pressing in the 13 underserved ZIP codes where we focus our free programs. These neighborhoods experience high rates of stray animals, pet surrenders, and dog bites, particularly involving children. Families here also face systemic barriers to care—from the cost of veterinary services to a lack of transportation and limited access to nearby clinics. Meanwhile, children regularly encounter loose or unsocialized dogs—while walking to school or playing outside—without ever having been taught how to safely respond.

That's the kind of scene—kids outside, unsure what to do when a loose dog approaches them—that should stay with your reader. It captures urgency, vulnerability, and mission in a single image. That's the power of story.

Train Your Team to Spot Stories

Your staff and volunteers are on the front lines. They see the transformations, hear the heartfelt thank-you's, and witness the everyday moments that make your mission real. But unless they know how to recognize and share those moments, powerful **Stories** will slip through the cracks. That's why it's so important to teach your team how to collect **Stories**—not just for newsletters and social media, but to fuel fundraising, build trust, and connect with your community.

Stories don't have to be long or literary to be powerful. They just have to be true. A good story connects a face with your work. It reminds people that this isn't just about numbers, but about lives changed. The best stories are short snapshots: a moment of transformation, a simple quote from an adopter, or a description of how your team helped an animal in need.

Start by focusing on the basics. *Who was helped? What was the situation before? What happened next? How did your organization make a difference?* Add a name, a photo if possible, and a real voice. Even one quote—from a foster, a client, or a vet tech—can bring a story to life.

It also helps to remind staff and volunteers that they don't need to write a polished article—they just need to capture a moment. A quote, a few quick details, or a short description is enough. Grant writers can shape the story later, but it has to be captured first. That's why it's important to teach them what to look for and what to ask. Make it easy for them to share what they see and hear. Then you can write the piece from those fragments, filling in the gaps and bringing the story to life.

#51: *Want More Stories? Teach, Model, Celebrate.*
Staff don't always like collecting stories—and it's not because they don't care. Often, they don't know how or why. That's why story collecting should be taught like any other skill. Model it. Make it easy. Use a simple form (paper or digital) that walks them through what to ask. Then show them where those stories go—in newsletters, social posts, grant reports—and how their words make a difference.

Want to take it further? Make it fun. Create a monthly drawing for stories that get featured. Celebrate a "Story of the Month" in team meetings. When staff see their stories being shared—and feel acknowledged for them—they start seeing and celebrating the stories all around them.

(Need help getting started? See Appendix 1: How to Access Your All-In-One Grant Toolkit for worksheets and templates you can download around story collection.)

#52: *Don't wait until the end of the year to collect Stories and Data.*
Add "story of the month" to your staff meeting. Pull one great quote from a client survey each quarter. Set up a shared folder where staff can drop photos and short client notes. When story-gathering becomes a habit, not a scramble, you're ready to meet your deadlines.

Why Data Matters

Stories make funders feel. **Data** makes them believe.

Good **Data** backs up your story. It proves your credibility. It shows you don't just have passion—you have results. You're not just doing good, you're making a measurable difference.

Funders want to know things like:

- How many animals or people you serve.
- What specific outcomes you achieve.
- How you measure success.
- That you have systems in place to track and report results.
- Community data showing areas with the highest shelter intake or pet surrenders.
- Percentage increase in services provided year over year.
- Repeat clients and follow-up rates.
- Number of children reached through humane education, including pre/post survey results.
- Cost-per-service (average cost to spay/neuter, vaccinate, or microchip).
- Time saved, clients transported, or geographic reach improved through mobile clinics.

For instance, if your program helped 7,500 families last year, break it down: 40% came from five ZIP codes with the highest shelter intake rates. That shows you're targeting the right areas—and your **Data** proves it.

Even the most moving story will fall flat if you can't follow it up with numbers that prove your impact. One funder told me, "I loved their story—but I couldn't tell if they were helping 10 people or 10,000." That's the gap you have to close.

How Stories and Data Work Together

Here's the real magic: **Stories** make your **Data** meaningful. And **Data** makes your **Stories** fundable. Let's say your program helps reduce shelter intake in high-stray areas through targeted spay/neuter. You could write: "We need $25,000 to provide 500 surgeries in 10 ZIP codes with high intake rates." It's clear, specific, and measurable. But what happens if you pair it with a story?

When we first met Luna, a stray shepherd mix, she was nursing her second litter of the year. A kind family had taken her in, but they couldn't afford veterinary care. They wanted to help—so we stepped in. Through our no-cost spay/neuter program, Luna received the care she needed. We also provided food, vaccinations, and supplies to support her and her puppies.

Luna is now spayed, healthy, and officially part of the family that rescued her. They found loving homes for all her puppies—and gave Luna a second chance at life.

But Luna's story is far from rare. In her ZIP code alone (78253), 327 unaltered dogs were surrendered to the shelter last year. We're working to reduce that number by providing free and accessible services in neighborhoods where families want to help—but just need a little support to do so.

Suddenly, your **Data** isn't just a number—it's a mission with a face.

Here's another example, short and to the point. *"Carlos brought in his elderly cat after she stopped eating. She had untreated dental disease. In just six months, our clinic saw 53 similar cases—all in the same low-income ZIP code. That's when we knew that dental care had to be next on our project list."*

#53: *Don't overthink the formula. Just pair one story with one strong statistic.*
You're not writing a novel or a research paper. You're building a case. When your emotion and evidence walk side by side, funders get the full picture: who needs help, why it matters, and how you're making a difference.

#26: *Make sure your story and stats work together.*
Ask AI to review what you wrote. If your story is about access to care, don't use adoption numbers—use data about transportation, affordability, or veterinary wait times.

#27: *Paste Stories and Data into AI and ask:*
"Help me write a grant paragraph that blends this story with these metrics to show need and impact." AI can help structure your content while keeping your voice intact.

Where to Use Stories and Data in a Proposal

Not every section of a proposal needs a story, so knowing where to place them can make all the difference. Here are some suggestions for potential story placement

- **Needs Statement:** Lead with a real-world story that reflects the broader problem. Then show the data.

- **Program Narrative:** Use **Stories** to illustrate how your services work in real life. Follow with metrics that show scale and reach.
- **Evaluation:** Share a story of someone who experienced a successful outcome. Then tie it to your outcome **Data**.

Stories and Data are allies. One inspires, the other reassures. One paints the picture, the other builds the frame. When you learn to use both—strategically and intentionally—you turn your grant proposal into something powerful: a document that not only gets read but remembered. And more importantly, one that's more likely to be remembered when the shortlist is made.

LESSON 8 Key Takeaways

- ☑ ***Stories** spark emotion, **Data** builds trust. Together, they connect and convince.*
- ☑ *A strong proposal needs both heart (stories) and proof (data).*
- ☑ *Teach staff how to collect **Stories** using a simple form—and share the stories back with them.*
- ☑ *Use real, relevant **Stories** that match your program goals and funder priorities.*
- ☑ *Back up every emotional appeal with measurable, specific **Data**.*

COMING UP NEXT In *Lesson 9*, we'll dig into your **Target Audience and Demographics** and explore what it really means to know who you serve.

LESSON 9

Target Audience and Demographics: Showing Funders Who You Serve

In the last chapter, we talked about the power of **Stories and Data** — how stories open the emotional door, and data gives your proposal structure and strength. Now, we're going to zoom in on one of the most important types of data: the numbers that describe *who you serve* and *why they need help*.

Before a funder gives you a dime, they want answers to two questions:

Who are you helping?
And how do you know they actually need help?

That's where **Target Audience and Demographics** come in. They go hand in hand — like a real-life story and the stats that back it up.

- **Target Audience** is the *who* — the people and pets your program is designed to help.
- **Demographics** are the *proof* — the numbers that describe their income, housing, access to care, and the systemic barriers they face.

When you put them together, you're not just describing a need — you're showing that your program is built to meet that need intentionally. That kind of clarity builds trust with funders. It says: *We know our community. We've done our homework. And we're ready to make a difference.*

Let's dive in and sharpen your **Stories** with **Data** that sticks.

Target Audience = Who You Serve

This is the group your program is designed to help. Describe them in a way that captures their situation, needs, and challenges.

Example: *We serve low-income pet owners in underserved Fort Worth neighborhoods who struggle to access veterinary care for their pets due to financial hardship, lack of transportation, or language barriers.*

Here are a few more examples of people you might serve:

- **Families in underserved ZIP codes with no nearby veterinary clinics**: These communities often lack access to affordable veterinary care, leading to untreated illnesses, unplanned litters, and increased shelter intake.
- **Seniors on fixed incomes who rely on their pets for companionship**: Many older adults struggle to afford rising veterinary costs and may forgo their own needs to care for their animals.
- **Individuals experiencing homelessness with pets**: People living on the streets or in shelters who depend on their pets for stability, safety, and emotional support.
- **Spanish-speaking or multilingual communities**: Pet owners who may face language barriers when accessing services, making it harder to get preventive care or understand their options.
- **Pet owners with financial hardship:** Families unable to afford vaccines, spay/neuter, or preventive care, often leading to avoidable health issues or relinquishment.
- **Owned pets without access to preventive care**: Pet owners who want to do the right thing but face barriers—like cost, lack of transportation, or limited clinic hours—that prevent them from getting their pets vaccinated or spayed/neutered.
- **Community cat caretakers**: Individuals doing their best to feed and protect unowned cats but lacking access to TNR (trap-neuter-return) programs or veterinary support.

The clearer your picture, the more funders can grasp the full scope of your work—and why it matters.

#54: *Know who you're helping and why they need your program.*
The more clearly you define your audience, the easier it is for funders to see how your program directly serves their funding priorities.

Demographics = The Proof

Once you've described your **Target Audience**, your **Demographics** profile fills in the details that help funders truly understand who you serve. This is where you move from general descriptions to hard numbers and specific characteristics that prove you know your community—and that your program is intentionally designed to meet their needs. Here are some questions you might ask:

- *Where do they live (ZIP codes, counties, neighborhoods)?*
- *What income levels or poverty rates exist?*
- *What languages are spoken?*
- *What barriers to care do they face (cost, transportation, hours, language)?*
- *What is the scope of the pet population (owned pets, strays, free-roaming cats)?*
- *Are there specific risk factors (high intake areas, dog bites, public safety issues, public health risks)?*
- *Are there cultural or trust barriers (fear of judgment, immigration concerns, prior negative experiences with services)?*

Example: *We serve low-income pet owners in five Fort Worth ZIP codes where 68% of residents live below 200% of the federal poverty level, 45% speak Spanish as a first language, and there is no full-service veterinary clinic within a 10-mile radius.*

#55: Remember, funders love Data.
It proves you know your community and what they need. Don't just guess. Find **Demographics** that speaks to your project.

Where to Find Demographics

Now that you know what **Demographics** are, let's talk about where to find them. You don't need a research degree—you just need to know where to look. The following sources will help you uncover the real numbers behind your target audience.

- **Census.gov (income, population, language spoken):** The U.S. Census provides basic data about population size, poverty levels, household income, and primary languages spoken — all of which help describe your target community.
- **City-data.com (community and neighborhood profiles):** A user-friendly site that breaks down city and ZIP code-level data like income levels, housing costs, education levels, and other social indicators. Great for narrowing in on your specific service area.
- **City or county shelter intake data (stray intake, owner surrenders):** Shows how many animals are entering local shelters, why they're being surrendered, and where they're coming from. This data helps you connect animal intake trends to human service gaps.
- **Community health assessments:** Often conducted by public health departments or hospitals, these reports provide insight into broader community health, including

income disparities, access to care, transportation challenges, and sometimes even pet ownership data.

- **School free/reduced lunch percentages (income proxy for families):** If census data feels too general, local school data offers a practical snapshot of economic need among families in your area. The percentage of children receiving free or reduced lunch correlates closely with poverty levels.
- **Public health department statistics**—Public health agencies often track zoonotic diseases (infections that can spread between animals and people), dog bite reports, and vaccination rates. They may also publish a community needs assessment annually that help you frame pet health issues alongside broader public health concerns.
- **Animal control call data (bite reports, loose dog complaints, neglect calls):** Animal control agencies track calls for service, providing insight into stray population hotspots, dangerous dog issues, neglect trends, and public safety risks—all of which can strengthen your case for prevention programs.
- **Transportation availability (public transit gaps):** Mapping how far your target audience has to travel for veterinary care—and what transportation options exist—shows whether distance and lack of transportation contribute to delayed care, unaltered pets, or emergency-only treatment.

#56: *Local Data = Local Credibility.*
Use **Demographics** from Census.gov and City-Data.com; studies done in your community, state or across the nation; and your local shelter's annual and quarterly reports in any part of the grant where you need to make the case for your programs. You don't need to use *every* data source you find, but pulling three to four solid, local data points creates a credible, funder-friendly case.

#28: *AI can help you with research.*
Think of AI like your GPS—great at getting you close, but sometimes it tells you to turn into a lake. Before you put any numbers in your grant, verify the source.

#29: *Let AI do the heavy lifting.*
Overwhelmed by pages of studies and **Data**? Upload your community reports, shelter stats, or Census data and ask AI to pull out key numbers that apply directly to your project. You can even ask: *How many people in my county are experiencing homelessness based on current data?* AI can scan public databases and studies across the Internet in seconds, surfacing the local stats you need to strengthen your grant.

BOOT CAMP SIDEBAR
Pulling It All Together

Let's take a closer look at how **Target Audience, Demographics**, and program **Data** work together in a grant proposal. Each section answers a different question, but all three need to align.

Example Target Audience Section

Our target audience is pet owners in underserved neighborhoods who want to care for their pets but struggle to access even the most basic veterinary services. Many families face multiple obstacles at once: transportation is limited or non-existent, the cost of care is beyond reach, and full-service clinics are miles away. As a result, routine wellness visits are delayed, treatable illnesses become crises, and pet owners are often left with the heartbreaking decision of surrendering a beloved pet when care is unaffordable or unavailable. These barriers don't stem from a lack of concern for their animals but from the absence of realistic options that match their circumstances.

In these communities, pets are often unvaccinated, unaltered, and untreated for common health problems, which contributes to higher stray populations, dog bite incidents, and additional strain on the local shelter system. The need is not only for affordable medical care but also for accessible services that meet people where they are—services that can prevent suffering, keep pets in their homes, and strengthen the bond between pets and the families who love them. By focusing on this audience, we aim to reduce unnecessary surrenders and create healthier, safer neighborhoods for both people and animals.

Evaluation of Target Audience Section

- Clearly identifies who you serve: pet owners in low-income, underserved veterinary deserts.
- Describes challenges: limited vet care, transportation, language, high strays, dog bites, surrenders.
- Humanizes the problem: families want care for pets but can't afford or access it.
- Links community needs to program solutions.

Example Demographics Section

The 10 ZIP codes we serve are among the most underserved in the region. More than 60% of residents live at or below 200% of the federal poverty level. Approximately 17%–21% live below the official poverty line—significantly higher than the state average of 14%. These neighborhoods are home to predominantly minority populations (up to 85%) and have a renter occupancy rate of over 90% of households are renters, indicating financial vulnerability and instability.

Language access is also a concern, with 45% of households speaking Spanish as a first language. Public transportation is limited, and there are no full-service veterinary clinics within a 10-mile radius of these neighborhoods. Combined, these factors present systemic barriers to care, contributing to preventable medical issues in pets and straining the local animal shelter system.

Evaluation of Demographics Section

- Provides specific data: poverty rates, minority percentages, housing instability, language barriers.
- Demonstrates urgency with comparisons to state averages.
- Ties demographics directly to why these neighborhoods are at-risk and underserved.

Let's Loop Back to Program Data

You might be thinking, *"Wait—didn't we already cover data in the last lesson?"* Yes, but now we're zooming in on how it works hand-in-hand with your **Target Audience** and **Demographics**. When you connect your **Program Narrative** with specific local statistics and real program results, you move from a heartfelt appeal to a funder-ready case. This is the kind of **Data** you can (and should) weave into your **Stories** and into your **Target Audience** and **Demographics** sections—wherever it makes the strongest impact.

Another example

Last year, we served over 1,400 pets through mobile clinics, transport programs, and outreach events in these 10 ZIP codes. Demand for services has grown more than 70% in the last two years. Currently, over 300 families remain on waitlists for spay/neuter surgeries, vaccinations, or basic veterinary care. Shelter intake and dog bite reports have remained elevated in these areas, further underscoring the need for community-based prevention and intervention services.

Short Versions for Tight Character Counts

Target Audience: *We serve low-income pet owners in 10 veterinary desert ZIP codes in [City/Region]. These families face barriers like cost, transportation, and language, leading to high rates of unvaccinated pets, strays, and shelter surrenders.*

Demographics: *More than 60% of residents live at or below 200% of the poverty level. Up to 85% identify as minority populations, and over 90% are renters. These ZIPs lack nearby veterinary care, public transit, and Spanish-language access.*

Data: *Last year, we served 1,400 pets. Demand has grown 70% in two years, with 300+ families still on waitlists for spay/neuter and vaccines.*

Need Super Short?

*We serve low-income pet owners in 10 veterinary desert ZIP codes (**Target Audience**)...where more than 60% live below 200% of the poverty level and have no full-service vet clinic within 10 miles (**Demographics**). Last year, we served 1,400 pets, and demand for services has increased 70% in two years (**Data**).*

#57: *Say who, say why, say what's at stake.*
Who? Low-income pet owners in underserved ZIPs. **Why?** Limited access to care + systemic challenges. **What's at stake?** Unvaccinated pets, owner surrenders of pets to shelters, and overwhelmed shelters.

#58: *Prove you know your audience.*
When you combine your **Target Audience** and **Demographics** into one compelling paragraph, you're not just answering the funder's question—you're proving you've done your homework. You're showing that you understand your community and designed your program *on purpose*, not by accident.

#30: *Use AI to find and format local demographics.*
If you don't have recent **Data** handy, ask AI to help. Try: *"What are the current race/ethnicity demographics for [ZIP code or city]?"* You can also paste in a Census table or city report and ask AI to summarize the key points. Then, double-check anything you include in a grant to ensure accuracy.

#31: *First, write long. Then edit for space.*
Word counts are shrinking, but your understanding shouldn't. Write the full version of your answer and save it in your grant folder. Then use AI (or your own red pen) to create shorter versions tailored for tight applications—without losing the substance.

LESSON 9 Key Takeaways

- ☑ *Funders need to know exactly who you serve—be specific, not generic.*
- ☑ *Your **Target Audience** explains who you serve and what challenges they face.*

- ☑ *Your **Demographics** provide **Data** that describes your audience and proves you know your community.*

- ☑ *Combine **Target Audience + Demographics** to create a full profile.*

- ☑ *Include both people and pets in your profile to show the full scope of need.*

- ☑ *Use real, local **Data** to back up your narrative—census, shelter intake, animal control, school data, public health, and transportation gaps.*

- ☑ *You don't need perfect **Data**—you need credible, relevant **Data** that paints a clear picture.*

- ☑ *The stronger your profile, the easier it is for funders to see how your work aligns with their priorities.*

COMING UP NEXT In *Lesson 10*, we'll dig into **Implementation and Timelines**—and how to show funders the steps you will take to complete this project.

LESSON 10

Implementation Plan and Timelines: Proving to Funders You Can Deliver

You've written your story. You've laid out your objectives. Now the funder's thinking: *"Sounds great… but can you actually pull this off?"*

This is your moment to prove you're not just dreaming big—you're delivering. Your **Implementation Plan** and **Timeline** are the blueprint that shows funders how the work gets done, who's doing it, and when. Funders don't just want a great idea. They want to invest in people who can bring it to life—step by step, on time, and on purpose.

This section answers one big question: *Do you have what it takes to make this happen?* For example:

- *Do you have the staff?*
- *Do you have partners to support the work?*
- *Are your logistics solid?*
- *Can you stay organized and meet your goals?*

Here is where many grant proposals stumble; not because the program isn't good, but because the plan sounds like it's being held together with good intentions and duct tape. You're not just telling a story anymore. You're handing over a roadmap and showing funders they can trust you to follow it.

This isn't the place for "trust us, it'll all work out." Funders don't fund hope—they fund preparation. Your **Implementation Plan and Timeline** must prove that you're capable, that you've got the know-how, and that you have a clear, step-by-step plan to roll it out. Let's break it down and build a plan that funders can believe in.

What's the Difference Between Implementation Plan and Timeline?

Here's how to think about the two:

▶ *Implementation Plan = Your Work Plan (The What and The How)*

This is your detailed, boots-on-the-ground description of how your program is going to run—from kickoff to wrap-up. It's like walking a funder through your game plan. This is more than just what you *hope* to do. It's what you're *ready* to do.

Here's what to include:

- **The steps you'll take:** Spell out the specific actions involved in delivering your program. *Are you hosting mobile clinics? Launching a foster recruitment campaign? Building a spay/neuter transport route?* Break it down. What happens first, second, third? Don't just say, "We'll expand services"—tell them *how*.

- **Who will do the work:** List your key players if they ask. Who's running point on each task—staff, volunteers, contractors, or partners? Show that you're not running this solo.

- **Where services will happen:** Be clear and concrete. Will this happen at your shelter, in targeted ZIP codes, online, or via mobile units? This grounds your proposal in a physical reality and shows that logistics have been considered.

- **What partnerships and systems are involved:** Mention your collaborators and any systems or platforms that support the work. *Are you partnering with community centers, vet clinics, or municipal shelters? Using an appointment scheduling system to manage outreach?* This shows you've built infrastructure and relationships to support success.

- **The sequence of activities:** This is where you show you've mapped the rollout. *What needs to happen before services begin? What's ongoing? What happens at the midpoint or year-end?* A logical sequence shows you've thought this through—and you're ready to go.

▶ *Timeline = Your Calendar (The When)*

Your timeline is the zoomed-out calendar version of your plan. It's a quick snapshot of when everything will happen—by week, month, or quarter. Some funders even ask for it in table or bullet form, so keep it simple.

Here's what to include:

- **What tasks will happen:** Convert your implementation steps into specific tasks with expected start and end times. Example: "Conduct neighborhood outreach," "Hire bilingual coordinator," "Host first foster orientation."

- **What happens first, second, third:** This is your logical flow. Don't say, "We'll evaluate the program" in Month 1. That comes later. Show you understand what must be done early (planning, outreach, staff training) vs. mid-stream (service delivery, data collection) vs. end-stage (reporting, follow-up, adjusting).

- **What key dates or quarterly phases can you provide:** Help funders orient themselves. Group tasks into quarters or months and align them with your fiscal/calendar year. Even approximate windows (Q1, Q2) can signal organization and readiness.

- **How will you know when you've reached a major milestone?** Include a few measurable points along the way. This could be "First clinic launched," "100 pets served," or "Partnerships finalized." Milestones are great markers for progress—and they let funders feel reassured you're staying on track.

A clear, realistic timeline shows funders that you've thought through not only what needs to be done, but also when and how it will happen. It signals organization, accountability, and the ability to follow through on your plan. By mapping out tasks, phases, and milestones, you help funders visualize your path forward.

Example Implementation Plan

In our mission to address the challenges faced by pet owners in underserved communities, we have developed a comprehensive implementation plan aimed at increasing access to essential veterinary care. Through targeted outreach, strategic partnerships, mobile vaccine clinics, our program endeavors to bridge the gap in pet care services, particularly in areas where barriers such as transportation challenges and limited access to veterinary care are prevalent. This outlines our approach to effectively implementing our program, emphasizing our commitment to promoting responsible pet ownership and improving the welfare of pets in marginalized communities:

- ***Identify Target Areas:** We will begin by identifying neighborhoods based on income levels, pet-related issues, and access to veterinary care. We use this data to pinpoint the areas of greatest need. Once identified, we develop a detailed plan addressing logistics such as scheduling, staffing, transportation, and equipment.*

- ***Build Partnerships:** We will determine if partnerships are needed to expand services in each neighborhood. We will reach out to stakeholders, including city council representatives, community leaders, and local businesses, to help promote the program and garner support.*

- ***Launch Outreach and Marketing:** We will promote upcoming clinics through multiple channels—social media, flyers, community events, and through partners like food banks and service agencies—to ensure pet owners are aware of the services available.*

- ***Deliver Services and Schedule Surgeries:*** *At the clinics, we will provide core services while also educating pet owners about responsible pet care and encouraging them to schedule spay/neuter surgeries to help prevent unwanted litters.*

Ongoing Monitoring:

We will continuously monitor the program, tracking attendance, vaccination rates, and spay/neuter scheduling. Based on current data, approximately 50% of pets arriving at these clinics are unaltered, and an estimated 75% have never received veterinary care beyond possible spay/neuter surgeries—highlighting a critical gap in preventive care.

#59: Avoid vague language.
Get rid of weak phrases like *"as needed," "as available,"* or *"we hope to..."* They make your proposal sound uncertain. Funders want clarity and confidence. Use strong, purposeful language instead—words like:

- "We will..."
- "Our team will implement..."
- "Services will begin by..."
- "We've secured partners to..."
- "The program includes..."
- "This initiative is designed to..."

(Check out Appendix 1 and how to access Your All-In-One Grant Toolkit to access Lesson 10: Implementation and Timelines; 10.5 Reference Guide—*Sharpen Your Grant Language* for more language tips.)

#60: Show them you got this.
A strong implementation section answers one simple question funders always have: "Do I believe this group can actually do what they say?" When your plan reads like the above, the funder's answer heads towards "Yes!"

#61: Write the plan, then follow the map.
Don't start with a blank timeline. Start with your **Implementation Plan**, then organize it by time.

#32: Need an Implementation Plan? Let AI help.
When you're mapping out your **Implementation Plan**, try feeding AI a simple list, like "Who will do the work, where it will happen, when it starts, and who your partners are."

Then ask AI: "Draft an implementation section for my grant proposal using this structure." This gives you a strong starting point you can fine-tune.

Example Timeline of Same Project

The following breaks down the full workflow—identifying neighborhoods, building partnerships, marketing, service delivery, and follow-up—showing funders that you've thought through every phase of the program. Use whatever format helps you demonstrate your readiness.

MONTHS 1–2

Planning, Site Selection, and Early Outreach

- Analyze data to identify target neighborhoods based on shelter intake, income levels, pet population, and access to veterinary care.
- Prioritize ZIP codes for clinics based on greatest need.
- Contact local businesses, community organizations, schools, and municipal partners to secure clinic sites.
- Complete site visits and confirm locations.
- Begin developing bilingual marketing materials (flyers, door hangers, social media graphics).
- Conduct early outreach with community leaders and trusted partners to build awareness.

MONTH 3

Launch Marketing, Finalize Logistics, Begin Service Delivery

- Launch full-scale marketing campaign across partner agencies, social media platforms, and neighborhood channels.
- Confirm staffing schedules, clinic workflows, and supply readiness.
- Begin the first round of mobile clinics in targeted ZIP codes.
- Provide core services (vaccinations, microchipping, parasite prevention, spay/neuter scheduling) to approximately 100 pets per clinic.

> **MONTHS 4–6**

Ongoing Clinic Operations and Outreach

- *Continue mobile clinics across remaining target neighborhoods.*
- *Maintain steady outreach to boost participation, focusing on underserved populations.*
- *Track data at each clinic, including pets served, services delivered, client demographics, and ZIP codes.*
- *Schedule follow-up spay/neuter surgeries as needed.*

> **MONTHS 7–9**

Program Monitoring and Mid-Year Assessment

- *Review clinic data to assess community response and vaccination coverage.*
- *Identify any gaps in participation and adjust outreach as needed.*
- *Conduct client satisfaction surveys to gather feedback.*
- *Hold staff and partner debriefings to ensure smooth ongoing operations.*

> **MONTHS 10–12**

Year-End Reporting and Program Adjustment

- *Analyze cumulative data for total pets served, surgeries scheduled, and vaccination impact.*
- *Prepare final reports for funders, stakeholders, and community partners.*
- *Adjust plans for future clinics based on data, feedback, and neighborhood needs.*
- *Continue adjusting the service delivery area (based on results) if demand remains high.*

#62: Show you are ready to roll.
Funders aren't just looking for your dream schedule—they're looking for operational readiness. If your program can launch services within 60 to 90 days of receiving funding, you show them you're organized and low risk.

#63: Plans change. Build in breathing room.
The best timelines aren't rigid—they give funders confidence you've thought through the steps and have allowed enough wiggle room for real-world adjustments. Life happens, right? Sometimes, you must adjust the plan. (If that happens, and it's a major shift that will impact how you deliver on your promises, let the funder know in real time. Don't suddenly spring it on them in your year-end report.)

#33: *Let AI spot gaps to keep you in sync.*
After writing your timeline, run it through AI and ask: *"Does this timeline logically flow from my implementation plan? Are the steps in sync? Are there any steps missing?"* AI can help you double-check alignment between your work plan and your calendar—especially when funders ask for these sections separately.

BOOT CAMP SIDEBAR
When Funders Ask for Implementation and Timeline Together

If a funder asks for both answers in the same question or section, put your Implementation narrative first. Then follow it with a simple Timeline that shows when everything will happen. Here's a look at what that might include:

Implementation and Timeline: Mobile Vaccine Clinics

To expand access to essential veterinary care in underserved communities, we will launch mobile vaccine clinics across targeted neighborhoods identified through intake data, income levels, pet population estimates, and veterinary care access. In Months 1–2, we will analyze data, select clinic sites, establish agreements with community partners, and begin bilingual outreach efforts with local businesses, faith leaders, schools, and food banks to build public awareness. Site visits will ensure the mobile clinic locations are safe, accessible, and logistically sound.

By Month 3, full-scale marketing and scheduling will begin, supported by finalized staffing, clinic workflows, and supply readiness. Mobile clinics will launch in the first target neighborhoods, providing vaccinations, microchipping, parasite prevention, spay/neuter scheduling, and pet owner education to approximately 100 pets per clinic. Clinics will continue monthly through Months 4–6, rotating through remaining high-need ZIP codes.

Throughout service delivery, we will maintain community outreach to maximize participation, especially among pet owners with limited access to care. Data will be collected at every clinic, tracking services provided, client demographics, and spay/neuter follow-ups. By Months 7–9, we will conduct mid-year assessments, review client satisfaction surveys, identify participation gaps, and adjust outreach as needed.

In Months 10–12, we will complete data analysis, summarize program outcomes, and prepare year-end reports for funders and partners. Adjustments for future clinic operations will be made based on program data, lessons learned, and continued community needs.

Need it shorter?

We will launch mobile vaccine clinics in targeted neighborhoods identified through data on shelter intake, income levels, pet population, and veterinary access. In the first two months, we'll finalize target ZIP codes, secure clinic sites with local partners, conduct site visits, and begin bilingual outreach through trusted community networks.

By Month 3, clinics will begin providing vaccinations, microchipping, parasite prevention, spay/neuter scheduling, and owner education to approximately 100 pets per clinic. Clinics will rotate through neighborhoods over Months 4–6, with continued outreach to maximize participation.

Throughout the year, we will track services delivered, collect client demographics, and monitor spay/neuter scheduling. A mid-year review (Months 7–9) will guide any outreach adjustments. Year-end analysis (Months 10–12) will summarize total services provided, assess impact, and inform plans for future clinics.

#64 : Match the details to the dollars.
Believe it or not, the stronger your implementation plan, the fewer words you need. A funder should be able to scan your full plan in under a minute and feel fully confident you're ready to go. But when funders are considering larger grants, they may expect a bit more detail. Always scale your answer to match the size of the ask—and the size of the space they have provided for your answer.

#34: Let AI help you trim copy without losing meaning.
Many funders now tell you exactly how much they want to read with strict word or character limits. Start with your full version. Then let AI help you condense it, always ask AI: "Is this fully answering the funder's question?"

LESSON 10 Key Takeaways

- ☑ *Funders don't just want good ideas—they want to see your plan to deliver results.*
- ☑ *Your **Implementation Plan** explains how you'll carry out your program step-by-step.*
- ☑ *Your **Timeline** maps out major tasks, deadlines, and staff or volunteer responsibilities.*

- ☑ *A strong **Implementation Plan** shows you've thought this through before the money comes in.*

- ☑ *Good plans build confidence. Great plans also show flexibility when the unexpected happens.*

- ☑ *Funders want to see your operations brain, not just your animal-loving heart.*

- ☑ *Strong implementation = easier evaluation later. If your plan is clear, it's much easier to measure and report on your success.*

COMING UP NEXT In *Lesson 11*, we'll tackle **Evaluation and Metrics**—how to show funders exactly how you'll measure success and track your results over time.

As a grant writer, you are proof that behind every successful program is someone who believed enough to ask.

LESSON 11

Evaluation and Metrics: Helping Funders See What Success Looks Like

You've told the story. You've shown the plan. Now comes the funder's final question: *How will you know if it's actually working?*

Welcome to **Evaluation and Metrics**—the part of the proposal where you prove you're not just busy, you're effective. This section gives funders confidence that you'll track what matters, adjust when needed, and report back with meaningful results. This isn't about having fancy research departments or complex studies. Funders simply want to know:

- *Are you tracking what you're doing?*
- *Are you measuring whether it's making a difference?*
- *Are you using that information to make the program better?*

You don't need perfect **Evaluation** methods. You just need reasonable, repeatable ways to track and report your results.

Before we dive too deeply into **Evaluation and Metrics**, let's connect the dots. Up to this point, you've focused on writing your **Project Narrative**, clarifying your **Goals**, and defining your **Objectives**.

Now it's time to shift from describing the work to measuring it. That starts with understanding what you're putting into the program—your inputs. These are your staff, volunteers, supplies, community partnerships, and current funding. Think of inputs as the raw ingredients. Your outputs are what you did with them. And your outcomes are what changed because of it.

This lesson will walk you through how to track that change and how to show funders you're paying attention to both reach and results.

Framing the Evaluation

Let's define the key terms that structure your **Evaluation** section. These concepts often overlap, but they each play a specific role in helping funders understand how you'll track your program's effectiveness.

Evaluation—This is the umbrella concept. It's the overall process of reviewing a program's effectiveness, asking: *Did it work?* and *How do we know?* It shows funders that you're committed to learning, adjusting, and improving.

Metrics—These are the specific data points you'll measure as part of your **Evaluation**. Think of them as your measuring sticks. **Metrics** typically fall into two categories:

- **Outputs**—The countable activities (e.g., clinics held, pets vaccinated)
- **Outcomes**—The results or changes caused by your work (e.g., fewer surrenders, healthier pets)

Together, these elements form the building blocks of your **Evaluation** plan. It's how you will understand, track, and improve your project or program over time. It all comes down to:

- What data you'll collect—Numbers served, participant feedback, changes in behavior or conditions.
- How you'll collect it—Sign-in sheets, surveys, clinic logs, public data, etc.
- When you'll review it—Monthly, quarterly, or year-end checkpoints.
- How you'll use it—For grant reports, program improvements, and future planning.

You don't need a team of statisticians or a complex formula—just a clear, common-sense plan to figure out if your program is working.

Outputs vs. Outcomes – What's the Difference?

Let's discuss the two most common—and most often misunderstood—parts of any evaluation plan: your outputs and outcomes. You'll need to include both in your proposal, but this part can be very confusing for new (and even experienced) grant writers. Here's how to look at them:

Outputs = What you did. These are the countable activities.

Example: *We hosted 10 clinics and vaccinated 1,000 pets.*

Outcomes = What changed because you did it. These are the actual results and impacts.

Example: *Stray intakes and dog bites decreased by 20% in targeted neighborhoods.*

If you're unsure, just ask yourself:

Did we do what we said we would do? ➔ Output
Did it make a difference? ➔ Outcome

Funders expect you to track and report both outputs and outcomes. The specific numbers and data points you use to measure them? Those are your **Metrics**.

#65: *When in doubt, remember this.*
An output is what you did. An outcome is what changed because you did it.

#35: *Use AI to strengthen your Evaluation section.*
Once you've written your **Objectives**, you can feed them into AI and Prompt: *"Draft a simple evaluation plan based on these objectives. Include metrics, both outputs and outcomes."* AI can help you tighten your **Evaluation** section and double-check that you're covering both what you'll do and how you'll measure it.

Example Evaluation Plan

Let's pull the plan together. Below is a sample **Evaluation** plan that pulls all those elements together in a clear, funder-friendly format. You'll see short explanatory callouts throughout, breaking down what each part is doing—and why it matters.

Project Summary

Our project provides vaccination and microchip packages to 1,000 pets through 10 mobile vaccine clinics, averaging 100 pets per clinic. Based on past data, approximately 75% of these pets have never received vaccinations due to financial constraints, transportation barriers, and lack of access to veterinary care. At least 50% will also need spay/neuter procedures, which we actively schedule at the vaccine events.

▶ *This is your project summary recap—a quick reminder of what you're doing and why it matters.*

Outputs (What You Do)

We will track the number of clinics held (goal: 10), the number of pets vaccinated (goal: 1,000), the number of pets microchipped, and the number of spay/neuter surgeries scheduled (goal: 100+). We'll also collect demographic information on pet owners served, including ZIP codes.

We'll track the:

- Number of mobile clinics held.
- Number of pets vaccinated.
- Number of pets microchipped.
- Number of spay/neuter surgeries scheduled.
- Pet owner ZIP codes and demographics.

▶ *Outputs are the countable actions you take—services delivered, events held, people or pets served.*

Outcomes (What Changes)

We expect this project to increase access to veterinary care in underserved communities, reduce stray animal intake and pet surrenders, decrease dog bites and other public health complaints, and improve the traceability of lost pets through microchipping.

We'll track the:

- Increases in veterinary access (via ZIP code trends and client reach).
- Reductions in stray intake in targeted ZIP codes.
- Reductions in pet surrenders.
- Decreases in dog bite incidents.
- Increases in return-to-owner rates due to microchipping.

▶ *Outcomes are the results of your work—the "so what" of your outputs. This shows your impact on the community.*

Data Collection (How We'll Collect It)

We'll collect data using tools already built into our workflow, including:

- Clinic sign-in sheets.
- Intake and appointment forms.
- Shelter/public health records.
- Demographic data by ZIP code.

▶ *Funders want to know how you're collecting your data—show them it's built into your everyday work, not an afterthought.*

Data Review (When We'll Review It)

We'll regularly review and reflect on the data we collect:

- **After each clinic**—Review attendance, services provided, and follow-up appointments.
- **Quarterly**—Summarize ZIP code coverage, surgery referrals, and participation trends.
- **Annually**—Analyze patterns in stray intake, surrenders, and dog bites in targeted ZIP codes.

▶ *A clear review schedule shows that you're not just gathering data—you're using it to improve your program in real time.*

Use of Results (How We'll Use It)

Evaluation results will be used to:

- Report on outcomes to funders.
- Improve clinic operations and staffing.
- Target outreach in high-need areas.
- Inform future program planning.
- Strengthen our community partnerships.

▶ *This answers one of the most important questions: Will you use the data to improve? It signals accountability and smart stewardship.*

A strong evaluation section shows funders that you're committed to learning, adapting, and making a lasting impact. Whether your goals are modest or ambitious, showing how you'll track outputs and measure outcomes gives funders confidence that their investment will lead to real, measurable change in your community.

#66: Don't try to predict the future—just show them you're paying attention.
Your **Evaluation** plan doesn't need to anticipate every possible outcome, but it should show that you're tracking both immediate activity and longer-term impact.

#67: Build your own Metrics library.
Every time you write an **Evaluation** plan for a grant, save it. Over time, you'll build your own master "**Metrics** library" you can pull from—and AI can help you tailor it to fit different funders.

#68: *Write the report before you need it.*

One of the most helpful things you can do is write your funder report *before* the grant is even awarded. Why? Because it forces you to clarify what success looks like, decide what data you'll need, and create a structure for tracking your progress. If you can't write the report now, your **Evaluation** section probably isn't specific enough yet.

Writing the report first helps you:

- Identify exactly what metrics you'll need to collect.
- Build a timeline for when and how data will be reviewed.
- Spot any gaps in your plan or logic model.
- Ensure you're setting realistic, measurable goals.

And later? It makes reporting so much easier. Instead of scrambling to remember what you promised, you're simply filling in the blanks. A good **Evaluation** plan is just a great funder report written in advance.

#36: *Use these AI prompts to help you draft or refine your Evaluation and Metrics section.*

Here are some sample prompts.

PROMPT 1 *Draft a simple **Evaluation** plan for a program that [insert short program description]. Include my outputs, outcomes, data collection, and use of results.*

PROMPT 2 *Based on the following objectives, help me write an **Evaluation** section with **Metrics** for a grant proposal: [insert objectives].*

PROMPT 3 *List possible **Metrics** we could track to measure success in a [insert type of program] project/program. Include both outputs and outcomes.*

PROMPT 4 *Turn this paragraph into a grant-ready **Evaluation** section with clear outputs, outcomes, and how results will be used: [insert **Project Narrative**].*

PROMPT 5 *I need help identifying qualitative and quantitative data to evaluate a [insert program/project name] program. Please include how I could collect this data and how to present it in a grant proposal.*

LESSON 11 Key Takeaways

- ☑ ***Evaluation*** *doesn't have to be complex. Funders just want to know you're paying attention to what works.*

- ☑ *Start with what you already track. Build your **Evaluation** plan around existing tools, forms, and data.*

- ☑ *Show both reach and results. Funders want to see the numbers (outputs) and the difference they made (outcomes).*

- ☑ *Metrics matter. They're the bridge between your story and your impact—make them specific and trackable.*

- ☑ *A great **Evaluation** plan becomes your future funder report. The clearer you are now, the easier reporting will be later.*

COMING UP NEXT In *Lesson 12*, we tackle the word that makes grant writers sweat: **Sustainability**. That's because a lot of nonprofit projects and programs don't generate income, so how will you keep your program going once the grant money runs out?

You are proof that words can change lives — and you write them every day.

LESSON 12

The Sustainability Question: Showing Funders Your Program Has Staying Power

You've written the story. You've built the budget. You've mapped out the timeline. You've even convinced the funder to love your idea.

Then comes that question at the end of the application: *"How will you sustain the program after grant funding ends?"*

Cue the internal panic. It's a tough question, but with a little planning, it's easier than you think.

Because let's be honest—most of what we do in animal welfare (and many other nonprofits) isn't *revenue-generating*. Free vaccine clinics, free spay/neuter programs, free TNR—none of these programs pay for themselves.

But **Sustainability** doesn't mean *fully self-funding your program*, though. It means you've thought carefully about where future funding could come from—and you have a plan to keep the project going.

What Funders Really Want to Hear

Funders can't fund you forever—and they understand your programs are not all revenue-generating. But they also don't want to feel like they're pouring money into a program that's going to collapse the moment their support runs out.

This is where many grant writers freeze.

When asked about **Sustainability**, too many people default to the answer that funders dread hearing:

"We plan to keep applying for grants."

Ding. Ding. Ding. *Wrong answer.*

Here's why: Grant funders aren't supposed to be your permanent funding solution. They want to see that you're building multiple pathways to keep your programs alive over time—and that you're not entirely dependent on them year after year.

When funders ask about **Sustainability**, what they're really asking is:*"How are you thinking beyond just my grant?"* Show funders you're thinking long-term—and not relying on them forever. That's your cue to talk about:

- Donor development.
- Corporate sponsorships.
- Individual giving programs.
- Community support.
- Fee-for-service models (when appropriate).
- In-kind donations.
- Partnerships that share resources or staff.

It's not about having every dollar locked in; it's about showing funders that you have a strategy to support your organization through other funding streams, that you're thinking ahead, and expanding your capacity. (See *Lesson 20*: Beyond Grants: Diversifying Your Funding Streams for a deeper dive into this topic.)

Where Sustainability Really Comes From

Here's where you build your **Sustainability** answer—and your long-term fundraising plan:

- **Ongoing Grant Funding:** Funders actually know that you'll need continued grant support. That's fine, as long as you're actively applying and not solely dependent on one funder year after year.
- **Individual Donors:** No funding stream is more flexible than individual donations. Build your base early. Every donor counts—monthly givers, one-time gifts, major donors, workplace giving—they all add up.
- **Corporate Sponsorships:** Businesses often want local community visibility. Many will donate cash, supplies, or services in exchange for recognition or partnership. And lots of people love animal causes!
- **Community Support & Events:** Grassroots fundraising—adoption events, auctions, fun runs, donation drives—not only bring in dollars, but also expand your donor base.

- **Partnerships:** Sharing resources with other organizations (spay/neuter clinics, shelters, municipal agencies) helps reduce costs and broaden impact.
- **Fee-for-Service Options:** Not everything needs to be free. Some organizations successfully add small fees for certain services, while keeping core services free for those who need them most.

#69: *Sustainability is a mix of resources, not a single source.*
The real magic is when you layer these together—building a funding "ecosystem" instead of relying on any one stream. **Sustainability** is like animal enrichment—variety makes the system stronger.

Example Sustainability Narrative

Let's take a look at how the **Sustainability** question can be addressed in a grant. You don't have to give all these answers. But one or two should resonate with you.

Sustainability: Given that the program relies on providing free services to underserved communities, sustaining it requires ongoing support from grants and donations.

▶ *Excellent setup. You've acknowledged the reality: this work requires ongoing external support—it doesn't pretend to fund itself. Now follow with a few of these funding sources in your plan.*

There are several strategies that can help ensure the long-term **Sustainability** of the project:

Grant Funding: *We will continue applying for grants from foundations, government agencies, and other funding sources that support efforts to improve animal welfare and community health.*

▶ *Yes. It's okay to include grants—just not as the only solution. This version names multiple sources and connects back to the mission.*

Corporate Sponsorship: *We will pursue partnerships with businesses and corporations interested in animal welfare or corporate social responsibility initiatives. These sponsors may provide financial support or in-kind donations to offset operational costs.*

▶ *A solid example of expanding beyond traditional philanthropy. Funders appreciate when you're actively cultivating relationships that can bring new resources or services.*

Individual Donations: *We are growing our individual donor base to contribute regularly to the program. This includes annual campaigns, donor appeals, and crowdfunding platforms to engage more supporters.*

▶ *This shows you're building community buy-in. Even small gifts, when consistent, create long-term impact.*

Community Support: *We are engaging with local communities to raise awareness of the program's impact and generate grassroots support. This includes community-led fundraising events, volunteer recruitment, and in-kind donations of goods or services.*

▶ *Excellent inclusion. Grassroots support builds long-term relationships and demonstrates local investment in the work.*

Partnerships and Collaborations: *We plan to develop strategic partnerships with other nonprofits, veterinary clinics, shelters, and community groups to share costs, expand reach, and strengthen outcomes. These collaborations increase efficiency and unlock shared funding opportunities.*

▶ *Smart. This shows you're not doing it alone—and that collaboration can stretch resources further.*

Fee-for-Service Models: *We are exploring ways to generate revenue through modest, sliding-scale fees for certain services. For example, while core services may remain free, optional or specialized care will be offered at reduced cost for those who can afford it, with proceeds reinvested into the program.*

▶ *A creative approach that demonstrates entrepreneurial thinking. Even partial cost recovery helps reduce dependency on donations.*

#70: *A mix of revenue sources shows you're thinking strategically.* Developing a diversified funding portfolio by tapping into various revenue streams like grants, donations, sponsorships, fundraising events, merchandise sales, and fee-based services reduces reliance on any single source of funding and enhances financial resilience. Funders love to see that you're not putting all your eggs in one basket. You don't need to list every category in your own proposal. Pick a few approaches that best fit your organization's situation and speak honestly about how you're building **Sustainability.**

What Funders Don't Want to See

- "We don't know how we'll sustain this program."
- "We hope additional grant funding will come."
- "We will fundraise (with no details)."
- "We're counting on this grant."

#71: *Don't write your Sustainability plan like a wish list.* Write it like a work plan. Show that you're actively building each piece now, even if it's still growing.

#37: *Here are some great AI prompts to help draft strong Sustainability answers:*

- **PROMPT 1** Based on this program description, draft a sustainability plan that includes grants, donors, corporate support, partnerships, and revenue diversification.
- **PROMPT 2** Rewrite this sustainability section to sound more funder-focused and long-term.
- **PROMPT 3** Summarize potential sustainability strategies for a free community veterinary program serving underserved pet owners.

BOOT CAMP SIDEBAR
Can You Raise Money on Social Media or GoFundMe?

The short answer? Yes—but it's a tool, not a full funding strategy.

Social Media Appeals

Platforms like Facebook, Instagram, and TikTok can be incredibly effective when you need to raise smaller amounts for urgent, individual cases, like when a dog is hit by a car, a kitten needs surgery, or a senior pet is taken in with severe medical needs. These kinds of stories grab hearts and make people give. You can often raise a few hundred to a few thousand dollars quickly if you have strong photos, a short compelling story, and frequent updates.

Social media is best used sparingly when it comes to fundraising. (*Check out Lesson 20, Beyond Grants: Diversifying Your Funding Streams for more on this topic.*)

GoFundMe & Crowdfunding Platforms

Many animal shelters use GoFundMe, SpotFund, and similar sites can help when you have a larger emergency or special circumstance that your regular donors may not be able to fully cover. Some examples may include:

- Major cruelty and seizures
- Natural disasters (hurricanes, floods, fires, tornadoes)
- Large-scale hoarding cases
- Facility repairs due to storm damage

These sites allow your organization to reach both local and national donors quickly—well beyond their normal mailing lists.

#72: Structure your social media appeal as a story.
These platforms work best when the situation is bigger and urgent, highly visual, and time-limited. Create a beginning, middle, and end: Here's the problem. Here's what we're doing. Here's how you can help right now.

#73: Crowdfunding is a tool, not a strategy.
Emergency fundraising is not a **Sustainability** plan, but using these platforms can absolutely supplement your long-term funding mix when you need extra help.

#38: Let AI draft your appeal, then edit to make it your own.
AI can help write your crowdfunding campaigns too! Prompt: *"Draft a 300-word GoFundMe appeal for an injured dog needing emergency surgery, based on this case summary."* Insert your case summary.

LESSON 12 Key Takeaways

- ☑ *Sustainability isn't magic; it's about diverse, layered funding streams.*
- ☑ *Funders want to see you're not dependent on any one source.*
- ☑ *Grants are part of Sustainability, but should not be your entire plan.*
- ☑ *Build individual donor support early in the life of your organization, it gives you more flexibility later.*
- ☑ *Partnerships, corporate support, and fee-for-service options strengthen your position. Go out and get 'em!*

COMING UP NEXT In *Lesson 13*, we wrap things up with a strong **Conclusion** because even if funders don't always ask for one, you'll be ready to close with confidence when they do.

LESSON 13

The Conclusion: What To Say When You've Said It All

I'm going to keep this lesson short—because your **Conclusion** should be, too.

Most funders don't ask for a separate **Conclusion**, but every so often you'll see a box labeled "Closing Statement" or "Final Thoughts." Whether requested or not, it's worth knowing how to end your narrative with confidence. You've walked the funder through your full story—now it's time to leave them with a strong closing that reinforces your case and invites partnership.

A good **Conclusion** does more than summarize. It's your last chance to:

- Reaffirm your alignment with the funder's mission.
- Restate the problem and your proposed solution.
- Emphasize the urgency or timeliness of your work.
- Highlight your readiness to act and deliver impact.
- Offer a quick reminder of your expected outcomes.

- Express sincere gratitude.
- Invite continued engagement (e.g., offer to provide more information).

Sometimes your **Conclusion** lives in its own section; sometimes it's simply the final paragraph of your **Project Narrative** or **Cover Letter.** Either way, keep it short—one to two paragraphs max. Your goal is to end with clarity, confidence, and momentum.

Example Conclusion

Thank you for considering our request to support mobile vaccine and microchip clinics in underserved neighborhoods. With your partnership, we will provide preventive care to 1,000 pets across 10 mobile events, helping families who face financial and transportation barriers get access to vital services for their pets. These clinics are ready to launch, and we are actively working with community partners to ensure high participation and long-term impact. Your support will allow us to reach the neighborhoods that need it most, reduce shelter intake, improve public health outcomes, and keep more pets safe and traceable through microchipping. We will also track outcomes and explore ways to sustain the program through additional partnerships and community support. We are deeply grateful for your consideration and welcome the opportunity to provide additional information or materials upon request.

(**Note:** For more examples, see *13.1 Conclusion Builder: Write a Strong Finish with "3 Take It Up a Notch Techniques"* in the Appendix.)

#74: *Fresh eyes may find what you miss.*
Before you submit your grant, have at least one or two other people review it, especially for larger requests. A second reader can catch typos, awkward phrasing, or missing pieces you've read too many times to notice.

#39: *Let AI be your final gut check, not your ghostwriter.*
Save your full grant application as a PDF, upload it to your AI tool, and ask: *Does this grant fully answer all the application questions? Are there any gaps or sections I may have missed?* AI won't catch everything, but it's a smart double-check before you hit submit. **Caution:** If you ask AI to review for completeness, it may try to rewrite large sections. Instead, ask for "suggestions only," so you can decide what to keep and what to ignore. The best grants sound like smart humans, not smart machines, so it's important to keep your organization's "voice" intact.

LESSON 13 Key Takeaways

- ☑ *Not all funders ask for a **Conclusion**, but you should know how to write one because it can become part of a **Cover letter** or your **Project Narrative**.*

- ☑ *A great **Conclusion** is short, sincere, and strategic. It restates the problem and solution, reminds the funder of your outcomes, and ends with gratitude and readiness to act.*

- ☑ *End with confidence, not just courtesy. A well-crafted **Conclusion** can strengthen your proposal and leave a lasting impression.*

- ☑ *Want to take it up a notch? Consider name-dropping key partners, reminding the funder of your track record, or subtly inviting next steps, especially when the relationship is new or the competition is tough.*

COMING UP NEXT In *Lesson 14*, we'll tackle the one-pager that makes your proposal feel personal—the *Cover Letter*. It's short, it's strategic, and yes, you should write it last.

The most powerful proposals don't just ask for money; they invite funders to be heroes in your story.

LESSON 14

The Cover Letter: Framing Your Case

The **Cover Letter** may be short, but it carries weight. It's often the first thing a funder sees, and remembers. It's often optional. But when it's requested, it matters.

The **Cover Letter** is your first impression – a chance to frame your request, show alignment, and offer a human voice before the funder opens your proposal. It doesn't need to be long. But it needs to be strategic.

So why is this *Lesson 14* and not *Lesson 1*? Because a great **Cover Letter** isn't the first thing you write, it's the last. Only after you've built your proposal can you introduce it with clarity and confidence.

A great **Cover Letter** doesn't repeat your proposal. It frames it. It gives your request a human voice. It offers a glimpse of the people behind the paperwork and reminds funders why your work matters.

What a Cover Letter Is

- A brief, professional introduction.
- A one-page overview of who you are, what you're asking for, and why it matters.
- A way to highlight something that might not fit neatly in your narrative (like a recent leadership change or a financial deficit you've resolved).

What a Cover Letter Is Not

- A copy/paste of your grant summary.
- A place for fluff or fancy words.
- An afterthought.

Your 4-Paragraph Cover Letter Strategy

A great **Cover Letter** follows a simple structure. Each paragraph has a specific job to do, and together, they frame your proposal in a clear, confident way. This isn't the place to restate your full narrative. It's your chance to introduce your request, show alignment, and invite partnership, all in one page.

To make the most of your **Cover Letter**, stick to a simple, proven structure. These four short paragraphs introduce your request, frame your impact, and show funders that you're thoughtful, aligned, and ready to deliver. Here's how to make each paragraph count:

Greeting: Address the **Cover Letter** to a specific person, if possible. Use their full name and title and double-check spelling. If no name is listed, address it to the grant manager, program officer, or the foundation's name (e.g., "Dear [Foundation Name] Grants Committee").

PARAGRAPH 1 **The Introduction:** Introduce your organization and clearly name the project or program you're requesting funding to support.

PARAGRAPH 2 **The Ask and The Impact:** State how much you're requesting and what it will fund. Briefly connect the request to your mission and the community need.

PARAGRAPH 3 **Connection and Confidence:** Mention any alignment with the funder's priorities, previous support, or shared goals. Briefly note your readiness, outcomes, or credibility.

PARAGRAPH 4 **Gratitude and Invitation:** Thank them for considering your proposal. Invite follow-up and express openness to providing additional information.

Signature: Be sure to include the signer's name, title, email, and phone number. If the letter is coming from your executive director or program lead, confirm their availability for follow-up.

Example: Mobile Clinic Cover Letter

Dear [Funder Name],

On behalf of (Insert Organization Name Here), thank you for the opportunity to apply for support for our 20XX Mobile Clinic Expansion Initiative. We respectfully request (insert amount) to support 10 mobile spay/neuter clinics in underserved neighborhoods across (insert city or geographic area), each reaching an average of 100 pets per clinic.

This project targets areas with high rates of animal overpopulation, owner surrenders, and low access to veterinary care. By bringing services directly to communities in need, we remove barriers and reduce shelter intake. This aligns with your foundation's commitment to accessible animal care and community wellness.

(Insert Organization Name Here) has a strong track record of delivering high-volume, low-cost services with measurable results. We are ready to launch the first clinic within 30 days of funding and anticipate reaching 1,000 pets through this initiative.

Thank you for your time and consideration. Please let us know if you need additional information. We appreciate the opportunity to partner in creating healthier communities for pets and the people who love them.

Sincerely,
Name of CEO, Executive Director, or Grant Writer

#75: Your Cover Letter is the voice-over for your proposal.
Don't let it sound like the legal department wrote it. Let it sound like you. Direct, clear, and confident.

#40: Draft your Cover Letter, than ask AI to improve.
"Can you polish this to sound professional but warm?" Use AI to trim, format, and improve tone without losing your voice.

LESSON 14 Key Takeaways

☑ *Not every grant requires a **Cover Letter** but when it does, make it matter.*

☑ *Use your letter to introduce, not repeat, your proposal.*

☑ *Show alignment, readiness, and gratitude in under one page.*

☑ *Keep a few templates in your digital folder that you can tweak quickly.*

COMING UP NEXT In *Lesson 15*, we'll pull together your **Supporting Documents** to show you're organized, credible, and ready to put grant dollars to work.

The best proposals strike a balance between heart and head, combining compassion with credible data.

LESSON 15

Supporting Documents: Showcasing your Readiness and Credibility

You created your digital files and organized your budgets.

You built your story bank and collected client impact **Stories**.

You gathered your **Data** so you know exactly what you're talking about.

You created your project budget, so you know exactly what funding you need—and what it's for.

You researched funders who fund your types of projects, created your **Grant Spreadsheet**, and mapped out deadlines.

You wrote your **Mission Statement** and **Organizational History**.

You nailed your **Needs Statement** and **Project Narrative**.

You crafted funder-ready **Goals** and **Objectives**.

You identified your **Target Audience** and backed it up with **Demographics**.

You mapped out your **Implementation** plan and **Timeline**.

You built your **Evaluation** and **Metrics** plan.

And you have written your **Cover Letter**.

You've done all the hard work and applied every tip. Your proposal is strong, clear, and compelling. Simply put: You rock!

Now it's time to back it up with **Supporting Documents** that show your organization rocks, too. These attachments won't move anyone to tears, but they *will* do something just as important:

- Verify your legal standing.
- Confirm your financial health.
- Show that your leadership is actively involved.
- Demonstrate your organizational capacity and systems.
- Reassure funders that their investment is in good hands.

#76: Your Supporting Documents send a message to funders.
It says, *"We're real. We're stable. We're organized. We're ready to handle your money."* Make sure everything is together and organized.

Supporting Documents

Here's a list of **Supporting Documents** commonly requested in grant applications. You won't need all of them every time, but it's smart to keep them ready. Save each document in your digital grant folder. Keep everything labeled and up-to-date and you'll be ready to attach what funders ask for—without scrambling at the last minute.

Legal & Organizational Documents

▶ *Include your IRS Determination Letter*
Your official 501(c)(3) nonprofit designation from the IRS. This proves you are legally eligible for charitable gifts and grant funding. Always include a clean, current copy.

▶ *List your Board of Directors*
Provide a list of your Board of Directors. Some funders may request contact information. Consider creating organization-based email addresses (e.g., jsmith@yournonprofit.org) to maintain professionalism.

▶ *Adopt a Non-Discrimination Policy*
Many funders require confirmation that your organization serves clients equitably, regardless of race, gender, religion, sexual orientation, or disability. Write this statement now, have it board-approved, and store it in your digital grant folder.

Financial Documents

▶ *Prepare your Organizational Budget (Current Year)*
Show all projected income and expenses for your nonprofit. Break down revenue by source (grants, donations, program income) and expenses by category (staff, programs, admin, fundraising).

▶ *Update your Year-to-Date (YTD) Financials*
Provide a snapshot of your financial status mid-year. Funders use this to assess if you're on track with your budget.

▶ *Build a Project/Program Budget*
Detail the costs of the project tied to your grant request. Funders cross-check this with your narrative—so they must align. This document should also be the first document your grant writer sees. A good budget can anchor the entire story.

#77: Don't let the project budget be an afterthought.
The first document a grant writer should have in hand is the project or program budget, but too often, it's the last thing created. That's backward. A solid, pre-planned budget guides the narrative, not the other way around. Encourage your organization to build out next year's organizational, program, and wish list budgets *before* the year ends. This gives you, the grant writer, a clear roadmap: what you need, what it costs, and what types of grants to pursue. Otherwise, you're left scrambling to reverse-engineer numbers to fit a proposal. That happens far too often, and rarely works out well. Here is an example of what one might look like:

Line Item	Budget Narrative
Program Manager: $45,000	This covers 50% of our Program Manager's salary, who oversees clinic scheduling, staff management, and community outreach.
Supplies: $5,000	Includes vaccines, syringes, microchips, and basic medical supplies for 10 mobile clinics.
Marketing: $2,500	Covers design and printing of bilingual flyers, posters, door hangers, and digital ads promoting the clinics.

▶ *Submit your most recent IRS Form 990*
Your public tax return outlines revenue, expenses, net assets, executive compensation, and fundraising costs.

▶ *Attach Audited Financial Statements (if available)*
These demonstrate financial stability and internal controls via an independent CPA review. Often required if your budget exceeds $1 million annually.

▶ *Provide a Balance Sheet (if no audit is available or separately requested)*
Offer a financial snapshot that includes:
- **Assets:** Cash, savings, property, investments.
- **Liabilities:** Loans, debts, unpaid bills.
- **Net Assets:** What your organization owns after liabilities are subtracted.

BOOT CAMP SIDEBAR
What's a Budget Narrative—and Why Do Funders Care?

When funders ask for a budget narrative, they aren't just looking for your financials. They want to read the story behind your numbers. The budget narrative walks funders through each line item and answers questions like:

- *Why does this expense exist?*
- *How did you calculate this amount?*
- *What does this cover?*
- *Who is being paid?*
- *How does this expense tie directly to the program?*

The budget narrative shows how every dollar connects to your goals, explains any big-ticket items, proving you're cost-effective (not wasteful), and reassures funders you've got the financial skills to handle their money wisely.

#78: Don't skip the story behind the numbers.
If your audit or balance sheet shows any red flags—like a deficit, sudden drop in revenue, or negative net assets—own it, explain it, and move on. That's where your budget narrative comes in. It's not just a formality, it's your chance to show funders you're responsible, transparent, and ready to manage their investment. Even if they don't ask for one, if you have something they will question, explain it somewhere in application. Use it to give context, clarify expenses, and highlight your financial strategy. Silence leaves questions. A clear narrative builds confidence.

Strategic Plans and Partnership Documents

▶ *Letters of Support or MOUs (Memoranda of Understanding):* Shows that you are collaborative in the community. Letters from partner organizations, city officials, or community groups showing you have external buy-in. The strongest letters describe actual collaboration, not just "we like this group." Ask partners for these at the end of every year for the coming year's grant writing efforts.

▶ *Strategic Plan:* Shows where your organization is headed over the next three to five years. Funders like to see that your request aligns with your larger vision for the organization.

Organizational Leadership Documents

▶ *Key Staff Resumes or Bios:* Short bios (1 to 2 paragraphs) showing relevant qualifications of program leadership and key staff.

#79: Keep short bios in your digital folder.
Keep short bios for your executive team and board saved in your digital folder. Write them *before* you need them—not the night before the grant deadline when half your board is on vacation.

▶ *Organizational Chart:* A visual showing your reporting structure. Helps funders see who's responsible for oversight. They don't ask for this much, but if they do, it helps to have it handy in your digital folder.

Optional, but Sometimes Requested

▶ *Annual Report:* Public snapshot of your impact over the past year. Include key metrics, success stories, photos, board list, financial summary. If you don't have one, create a one-pager at the end of the year that highlights your accomplishments.

▶ *Insurance Certificates:* Proof of general liability, worker's comp, or other coverage (sometimes required for capital or facility projects).

▶ *Program Flyers, Brochures, or Media Coverage:* Helpful if funders allow optional attachments. Choose clear, recent materials that visually showcase your work.

▶ *Photos:* High-quality images of your programs in action. Select photos that highlight impact, diversity, community engagement, or transformation. Avoid cluttered or outdated images. Each photo should tell a story.

#80: *Create one master "Grant Attachments File" in your digital folder.*
Every time a grant opportunity pops up, you're ready with your **Supporting Documents**. Label everything with clear, consistent filenames, so it's easy for funders to pull and read. (*Example: ABCShelter_BoardList_2025.pdf*)

#41: *Use AI to clean and polish attachments.*
Paste a messy board list or budget into AI and ask it to format and label clearly. Use AI to rewrite dry bios into stronger, funder-ready staff profiles. Let AI double-check that your program budget aligns with your narrative.

LESSON 15 Key Takeaways

☑ *Funders use **Supporting Documents** to verify your nonprofit status, financial stability, leadership, and organizational readiness.*

☑ *Keep your **Supporting Documents** in your digital file folder so you're always ready to submit.*

☑ *Always double-check that your financial attachments match the numbers you included in your **Project Narrative** and Budget.*

☑ *Customize attachments for each funder, include only what they request (but be ready with everything).*

☑ *A clean, well-organized set of **Supporting Documents** sends a strong signal: We are organized. We are stable. We are ready.*

COMING UP NEXT In *Lesson 16*, it's time to cross the finish line. We'll cover **Proofing, Reviewing, and Submitting Your Grant**, so your proposal lands exactly where it should.

LESSON 16

Final Review: Proofing, Polishing, and Submitting Your Grant

Back when I first started writing grants, there were no online submissions. You printed everything—five complete copies, no staples allowed. Every set had to be perfectly collated, bound with a rubber band, and packaged in a folder or envelope. Some funders even requested color-coded tabs or specific hole-punch spacing.

It was time-consuming to handle.

Today's online portals may make grant submissions easier and more efficient to submit, but that doesn't mean the details matter any less. How you finish, and how you follow up, still shapes how funders see you—and it can absolutely impact your chances the next time you apply. This part isn't glamorous, but it matters.

Submit Everything Exactly as Requested

Follow the funder's instructions *exactly*. If they want one PDF, don't send ten attachments. If they say, "*submit through our online portal*," don't email your files.

Before you click submit, double-check:

▶ *File format (PDF, Word, Excel?):* Give them what they asked for.

▶ *File names (clear, professional, consistent?):* Don't submit something labeled "056434.pdf." Rename it to something like "HS-2025_Org_Budget.pdf." Use a consistent naming format across all your documents. Small details matter.

▶ *Is your organization's name on every file?* Add it to the top of every document—consistently and clearly. If the funder prints things out (and many still do), make it easy to see who they're reviewing. I've seen project budgets with no organization or program name—don't make reviewers guess.

▶ *Order of documents:* If the funder asks for a specific order, honor that request.

▶ *Cover letters or extra materials:* If they ask for a **Cover Letter**, provide one. If there's a chance to include one more attachment, include an annual report or a photo. Every piece contributes to your image.

▶ *Deadline time zone:* Note the exact day, time, *and* time zone the grant is due. (Trust me, time zones trip people up.)

And don't wait until the last hour to submit your grant. Online servers can crash. Portals can freeze. Submitting your grant early shows you're organized and respectful of their time.

#81: *Set a "safety deadline" that's at least 48 hours before the real one.*
This gives you a cushion for last-minute tech issues, internal reviews, or the random printer jam that always seems to strike at the worst moment.

Proof Like a Professional

At this point, you've read your proposal so many times your eyes are crossing. But this is your moment for a final, critical review.

- **Read it aloud.** You'll catch missing words, repeated phrases, and clunky sentences you didn't notice on screen.
- **Verify your numbers.** Make sure your narrative, budget, and attachments all match.
- **Get fresh eyes.** Have someone unfamiliar with the project read it. If they don't understand your main message, chances are a funder won't either.

#42: *Use AI for one last polish.*
Paste in your draft and ask: *"Does this section flow clearly, or are there parts that could be confusing or redundant?"* It's not a substitute for your judgment, but when you've been staring at the same text for hours, a fresh (digital) perspective can catch what you've missed.

Keep a Record of Everything

After you hit submit, take a few minutes to organize your files.

Update your **Grant Spreadsheet** with:

- Submission date.
- Amount requested.
- Project or program name.
- Notes on login credentials or funder communications.

In the same digital file folder, create a folder for that funder and save:

- A full copy of your final application.
- Submission confirmation (screenshot or email).
- All documents you submitted (or at least a list of attachments).

You'll thank yourself when it's time to report or reapply.

Follow Up Like a Pro

Hitting submit isn't the end of the process—it's just the next step. Most funders take six to eight weeks to respond. Some take six to eight months (yes, really). Unless otherwise noted, be patient, but don't go silent forever. If you haven't heard back after six months, send a short, polite email:

Just checking in on our submission to [Funder Name] sent on [Date]. Please let us know if you need anything further to make your decision. Thank you again for the opportunity.

Say Thanks When You Can

Regardless of their answer, send a thank-you, if possible. It's always good practice to express gratitude, even if your proposal wasn't funded. A simple thank-you reinforces professionalism and keeps the door open for future opportunities. If you have a contact name or email, you could send the following:

Thank you for the opportunity to submit a proposal. We appreciate your consideration and the work your foundation does for [community/cause].

#82: *Funders remember good manners.*
A thank-you—even after a rejection—shows you're professional, respectful, and in it for the long haul.

Occasionally, sending a thank-you isn't possible:
- If the application was submitted through a no-reply portal with no staff contact.
- If the funder explicitly states not to follow up.
- If the organization is anonymous or uses a third-party administrator with no clear contact.

When that's the case, let your proposal speak for itself.

Ask for Feedback (When Appropriate)

If the answer is no, consider asking for feedback—especially on larger or high-effort proposals. But use your best judgment. Some funders receive far too many applications to offer individual comments. You're more likely to get useful feedback from a community foundation where you can build a relationship with the staff than from a national funder that may be too overwhelmed with applications to reply.

When in doubt, a polite, one-line ask won't hurt: *If you're able to share any feedback, I'd greatly appreciate it for future submissions.*

And if you don't hear back, move on. Focus your energy on the next opportunity. A "no" (or no response) is never the end, it's just part of the process.

#83: Rejection doesn't mean your program isn't strong.
It just means this wasn't the right fit at this time. Keep going. Your next "yes" might be just around the corner.

LESSON 16 Key Takeaways

- ☑ **Follow instructions exactly.** *If the funder says combine all documents into one PDF, give them one PDF.*

- ☑ **Double-check file names, formats, and order.** *Make sure your documents are easy to read, review, and remember. Make all the file names uniform.*

- ☑ **Don't wait until the last minute.** *Submit early to avoid tech glitches, stress, or missed deadlines.*

- ☑ **Proof like a pro.** *Read your proposal aloud, double-check your numbers, and have someone else review it with fresh eyes before you hit submit.*

- ☑ *Use AI as your backup editor. It can catch small issues and help you clean up language before you hit submit.*

- ☑ *Save everything. Keep a copy of the final proposal, submission confirmation, and all attachments in a funder folder in your digital folder.*

- ☑ *Track your submissions. Update your* **Grant Spreadsheet** *with dates, amounts of request, and notes.*

- ☑ *Follow up with grace. If you don't hear back by the expected date, check in politely.*

- ☑ *Always thank the funder—win or lose. Gratitude goes a long way, and feedback (if they offer it) is priceless.*

COMING UP NEXT In *Lesson 17*, we'll talk about the hardest part of grant writing—**The Rejection**—and what to do when the answer is no.

Good proposals inform.
Great proposals inspire.

LESSON 17

The Rejection: Understanding Why You Didn't Get Funded (and What to Do About It)

You followed the formula, hit submit, and crossed your fingers.

Then you waited… and waited… and waited.

Until finally, the email arrived.

"Although your proposal has merit, please understand that the decision reflects the interests of the Charitable Trust, the high number of requests we received, and the amount available for distribution this year."

Oof. We've all been there.

Welcome (if we can call it that) to one of the most frustrating – but most important – parts of grant writing: The **Rejection**.

The good news? **Rejection** isn't failure; it's feedback. If you learn how to read between the lines, every "no" can help shape your next "yes."

The bad news? You'll get plenty of chances to practice.

This lesson is about turning that sting into strategy, so you come back stronger, smarter, and more prepared next time.

Why Was My Grant Declined?

Most funders won't tell you exactly why your proposal wasn't selected. They are too busy, and they have likely reviewed hundreds of grants. But there could be several reasons, so let's break it into two buckets:

▶ *Things You Can Control*

- Your proposal didn't align tightly enough with the funder's priorities.
- The story lacked clarity, urgency, or emotional pull.
- Your **Goals** or **Objectives** were vague or unmeasurable.
- The budget didn't match the narrative or felt unrealistic.
- Key partnerships or collaborations were missing.
- Some required attachments were missing or incomplete.
- You missed a deadline or failed to report on a past grant.
- Your data didn't fully support the need you described.
- The proposal wasn't tailored to the specific funder.
- You relied too heavily on AI and the result felt generic.

▶ *Things You Can't Control*

- There were more strong applicants than money to go around.
- The funder shifted priorities mid-cycle.
- Foundation leadership or board turnover paused new funding.
- The funder had less money to give out this year.
- They prioritized returning grantees with established relationships.
- Your organization felt too new or unproven (many funders prefer a three-year operating history).
- Unspoken preferences (familiar leadership, local ties, etc.) played a role.
- Local or national politics influenced decisions.
- External events (media coverage, economic shifts, community pressures) shaped outcomes.

When so many factors are outside your control, it can feel discouraging. But rejection doesn't always mean you did something wrong. Sometimes, it just means the competition was fierce, the timing was off, or the funder had to make hard choices. In a field like animal welfare, where many large cities now have multiple groups applying for the same limited pool of funding, even strong proposals get turned down. More groups = more proposals = more competition.

The takeaway? Keep improving, keep aligning, and keep applying. A no today doesn't mean no forever.

#84: *Track every Rejection in your Grant Spreadsheet – and the reason why, if you know.*
If the funder says they're a small foundation with limited giving, that may be a hint that your $5 million organization isn't the best fit for their priorities.

#43: *Use AI to help analyze what might have gone wrong.*
Paste in your proposal and the funder's guidelines, then ask in these instances: *"Where are the misalignments between this proposal and the funder's priorities?"* Just remember: AI won't always catch when the language feels too generic, especially if it was written by AI in the first place. Human editing still matters.

Your Post-Rejection Playbook

❶ Re-Read the Funder's Guidelines.

Start by going back to the original application. With fresh perspective, ask yourself honestly: Were we truly a strong fit, or did we stretch to make our project align with their priorities? Sometimes, we fall in love with our idea and hope a funder will too, but that hope needs to be backed by alignment in mission, goals, and target population. If the fit wasn't there, consider that a part of your learning curve, not a failure.

❷ Audit Your Proposal.

Review your proposal with a critical eye. Was your story clear and emotionally compelling? Did your goals and outcomes reflect measurable change? Did the budget support the story you told—and was it realistic? Were all required attachments complete, current, and labeled correctly? Did you fully answer every question in the application, not just provide general information? A checklist audit like this can help you spot holes that may have weakened your application (See Appendix 1: How to Access Your All-in-One Grant Toolkit, Lesson 17: 17.2 Checklist—Post Rejection Playbook).

❸ Step Away for Two to Three Weeks, Then Re-Read the Proposal.

Time gives you distance—and distance gives you objectivity. When you return to the proposal after a few weeks, read it as if you're the funder seeing it for the first time. Would you feel confident funding it? Does it inspire trust? Does the story grab you in the first few lines, or does it meander? This mental shift often reveals weak spots you couldn't see while working under deadline.

④ Ask for Feedback but Be Strategic About It.

Not every **Rejection** warrants a follow-up. Focus your feedback efforts on major funders like PetSmart Charities, Petco Love, Best Friends, ASPCA, or local foundations with whom you hope to build a long-term relationship. For smaller banks, family foundations, or charitable trusts, assume the **Rejection** was due to high demand, not a fatal flaw. Even a sentence like "*We had many strong applicants and limited funds*" tells you exactly why you were declined – too many applications, not enough money to go around. Your proposal may have been solid, just edged out by volume. That's not a failure. That's just math.

⑤ Revise Intentionally.

Rejections are an opportunity to refine a grant, so use them to write the next one or to resubmit a revised one to the same funder next year (if you think they liked the project). But never resubmit the same exact grant to the same funder that declined you. Even if your grant was strong and it was just math, you should always freshen a grant with new language, updated **Data** and new **Objectives**. Tighten your alignment to the funder's current goals (which may mean pitching a new project) because that can change annually too. Even small improvements to clarity, structure, or tone can make a big difference the next time around.

⑥ Track Patterns.

Use your **Grant Spreadsheet** or grant software to record outcomes. Which funders reply? Which don't? Which door should be opened for a second try? Over time, you'll see where your voice resonates, and where it doesn't. That knowledge helps you prioritize future applications and spend your time where it counts.

⑦ Celebrate Small Wins.

Not getting funded doesn't mean your effort was wasted. Small wins often come quietly— an invitation to reapply, making it to the final round, receiving a personal note from the funder, or even a request for more information. These signals mean your proposal stood out, even if it wasn't selected. They're signs that you're building visibility and trust. Take time to reflect on what you think worked and what you would tweak next time. Every submission sharpens your skills and brings you one step closer to a yes.

Reality Check: Even When You Do Everything Right...

You won't win every grant. No one does.

- Even experienced grant writers don't have a perfect track record—especially when the project isn't tightly aligned with the funder's goals.

- Newer grant writers may start with lower success rates (10–30%) as they build skills and relationships—but a strong, well-matched proposal can still win.
- Many funders won't award large grants to first-time applicants or all-volunteer organizations. It can take two to three submission cycles before a funder says yes, especially with national foundations. If you haven't been on their radar, they are going to wait a year or two to see what you are doing.

The goal isn't a perfect batting average. The goal is steady growth: sharper proposals, better alignment, stronger funder relationships, and clearer positioning with each grant cycle. That's what builds long-term success.

#85: Still think the funder's a good fit?
Pull their IRS Form 990 and see who they've funded, how much, and for what. Maybe you asked for too much, or they weren't confident you could deliver with less.

#44: Let AI be your post-game replay.
AI won't take **Rejection** personally, but it can help you learn fast. Attach your application and try these prompts:

- *"Compare this proposal to the funder's guidelines and suggest improvements."*
- *"Rewrite this proposal to better align with a funder that prioritizes underserved communities."*
- *"Identify weaknesses in this rejected proposal and suggest improvements."*
- *"Rewrite this section to emphasize urgency, measurable outcomes, and funder alignment."*
- *"Find 5 other funders who support this work in [state or issue area]."*

LESSON 17 Key Takeaways

☑ ***Rejection isn't failure; it's feedback.*** *Learn from it, revise, and come back stronger.*

☑ ***Some reasons are within your control:*** *misalignment, unclear goals, missing attachments, or a generic tone. Some reasons aren't: limited funds, unspoken preferences, or stronger applicants. It's not a reflection of your work.*

- ☑ **Track every Rejection.** Log the reason (if known), funder details, and any notes in your **Grant Spreadsheet**.

- ☑ **Never resubmit the same proposal.** Use each **Rejection** as a chance to revise and realign a proposal.

- ☑ **Ask for feedback, respectfully.** Even a simple response can give you useful insight.

- ☑ **Watch for patterns.** Over time, you'll see which funders are a good match for your mission.

- ☑ **Celebrate small wins.** Being invited to reapply or making it to a final round is real progress.

- ☑ **Use AI to review and refine.** Post-rejection is a great time to ask AI for suggestions and alignment checks.

- ☑ **Expect Rejection – and keep going.** Even top professionals don't win them all. The goal is improvement, not perfection.

COMING UP NEXT In *Lesson 18*, we'll talk about what happens when you get funded ((woohoo!),. from **Grant Implementation** and **Reporting Essentials**, we will cover what it means to keep the funder informed and happy.

LESSON 18

Grant Implementation and Reporting Essentials: Keeping the Funder Informed (and Happy)

Woohoo!!! You got the grant!

Take a moment to soak it in! Break out the treats! Notify the team! Ring the bell! High five your office dog or cat!

Just don't get too comfy...because now the real work begins.

When a funder gives you the green light, it's time to deliver on everything you promised, and show the funder they made the right call. The funder is saying: *"We believe you'll do what you said you would"*. Your job is to prove them right, with solid implementation, transparency, and on-time reporting.

Implementing the Grant

This is where good grant writers become great project managers. Don't let the grant sit quietly in the background collecting dust. While it may not be your job to run the project, it *is* your job to manage the grant. You are the grant's advocate from beginning to end – tracking progress, catching delays, and keeping the team aligned so your project has impact. That means making sure every promise made in the proposal is fulfilled, every person knows their role, and every piece of the plan is set in motion. If you said you would launch a program in September, don't wait until August 31 to get started.

- Set up the structure.
- Assign roles.
- Order materials.
- Meet with staff to review the timeline and metrics.
- Build excitement with the team.
- Set expectations with the team.
- Launch the project.

(Check out Appendix 1: How to Access Your All-in-One Toolbox, Lesson 17, 17.1 Checklist and Worksheet: Grant Implementation and Reporting in the downloadable materials.)

#86: *Print your original grant.*
Print your original grant and highlight every promise, then turn those promises into a checklist. Add dates. Add names. Add reminders. It's your accountability roadmap. And don't forget the human side. Funded programs often involve multiple departments — the clinic, outreach, admin, and volunteers. Keep everyone in the loop with mini updates, quick huddles, or a shared tracking document. The smoother your internal coordination, the better your external results.

#87: *What if things aren't going to plan?*
If something's not working, adjust early and write it down, so you're ready to explain later. But if something bigger throws off your plan, reach out to the funder. They'll often work with you to adjust timelines, shift deliverables, or find a solution that keeps the project on track. Honest updates build trust. Staying silent doesn't.

The Report: More Than a Recap

A grant report is your "*we did what we said we would do*" moment. It's not just a formality or a recap of your year. It's your chance to show what happened, how it went, and what impact the funding made. Think of your grant report as a highlight reel mixed with evaluation and metrics—showing what happened, what worked, and why it mattered.

Some funders give you a formal template. Others send a short list of questions. Occasionally, the only notice is a line in your contract saying a report is due in 12 months. No matter how it's framed, here's the bottom line: **grant reports are not optional.**

Most reports are due 6 to 12 months after the grant is awarded. Some require mid-year or quarterly updates. You won't always get reminders, so staying on track is on you.

#88: *As soon as your grant is approved, mark the report deadline on your calendar.*
Then add reminders at 90, 60, and 30 days out. A late report doesn't just make you look sloppy; it can cost you your next grant.

What Goes into a Grant Report?

Most funders will tell you what they want, but sometimes you have to read between the lines. Here's what they usually mean (and how to give them exactly what they're looking for):

▶ *Program Overview:* Start with the basics. What did the grant pay for? When did the work happen? Did anything shift from the original plan or timeline? Give them a clear snapshot of the program in action.

▶ *Goals and Outcomes:* Show your results. What did you set out to do, and did you do it? Revisit your original goals and include the metrics you promised. Numbers matter. Even if you didn't hit every target, be honest and explain why.

▶ *Impact Stories:* Put a face to the funding. Share a story about one animal, person, or community moment that brings the grant to life. Add a quote or photo (with permission). Keep it short but powerful. Make it memorable.

▶ *Challenges and Lessons Learned:* Be honest about your challenges. Funders understand that things can happen to derail your project or program. What matters most is how you respond, with early communication, transparency, and problem-solving. *What went well? What challenges did you face? What did you do to fix them?* Share how you adapted and what you would do differently, if applicable. Funders appreciate honesty and smart course corrections.

▶ *Financial Summary:* They want to know how the money was spent. Include a simple breakdown: budget vs. actual. Explain any big changes or savings. Confirm that the funds were used as promised. Keep it clean and transparent.

▶ *What's Next?* End with momentum. Will the program continue? How will you sustain it or grow it? Are new partners or funders coming on board? This is your chance to show long-term impact and invite future support.

#89: Remember that digital folder you created?
Now's the time to use it. Open it up, and pull your stats, quotes, photos, and stories. If you've been updating it throughout the year, more than half your report is already done.

#90: Keep your funders – and your team – in the loop.
A quick quarterly email with a stat, a story, or a photo is like a little *"Hey, look how great we're doing!"* wave from across the funding universe. But only wave at the ones who want to be waved at. If your funder prefers peace and quiet, respect that. No reports due for months? Write quarterly updates for yourself anyway. "Future You" will thank "Past You" for being so on top of everything.

#45: AI is your reporting and editorial assistant.
Let AI give you a first draft to polish or help you spot gaps you missed. Try these prompts:

- "Turn these program notes into a short funder report."
- "Rewrite this section to highlight impact and gratitude."
- "Draft a funder thank-you letter with our program update."
- "List the most common elements funders expect in a 12-month grant report."

The Best Way to Win Your Next Grant?

Do an excellent job with the one you have.

I've seen funders increase support and renew grants without a new application, based solely on a strong grant report. When they see their dollars used responsibly and making a real impact, it builds confidence, and makes them want to be part of your successful project.

#91: Don't disappear after the check clears.
Stay visible. Invite funders to events. Share quick updates and small wins. Ask if they manage other giving opportunities. A great report starts a relationship, but it's how you show up afterward that keeps it going.

BOOT CAMP SIDEBAR
Do I Need a Relationship with the Funder?

One of the most common questions I get: *Do I need a relationship with the funder?* The answer: *It depends.*

- *Some funders don't want one.* Think bank-managed foundations or family trusts with third-party administrators. These groups often avoid contact — and that's okay. Just write the strongest proposal possible.

- *Major local funders often welcome it.* Community foundations and corporate giving programs may invite a site visit, a meeting, or a conversation. Relationships help funders feel connected, but conversations don't guarantee funding.

- *National funders often expect it.* Many large funders reserve big grants for organizations they know and talk to regularly. Build those relationships by attending conferences, attending their webinars, or setting up short check-in calls to stay on their radar. Be patient. Visibility builds trust, and trust takes time. One group I coached didn't receive any funding during their first year writing grants, even though they had been around for 20 years. Once they started applying regularly and funders got to know them, the grants started rolling in.

#92: If the door's open, step in.
You don't need personal connections to every funder, but when opportunities for dialogue exist, take them. Every meeting, email, or site visit builds your reputation as a reliable partner.

LESSON 18 Key Takeaways

☑ *Winning the grant is just the beginning; now prove you're a great partner.*

☑ *Report on time. Early is even better.*

☑ *Keep your digital folder updated to save time on reporting later.*

☑ *Communicate early when plans change. Don't surprise the funder.*

☑ *Your grant report should include **Data** and **Stories**.*

- ☑ *Stay in touch throughout the grant, if they are open to it, not just at the end.*
- ☑ *Funders remember who made it easy to say "yes" again.*
- ☑ *Strong reporting leads to future funding.*
- ☑ *Relationships matter, especially with large community foundations and national funders.*

COMING UP NEXT In *Lesson 19*, we'll pull back the curtain on **Using AI in Grant Writing**. You'll learn how to save time, reduce stress, and make your proposals even stronger…all without losing your voice or compromising your message.

LESSON 19

Using AI in Grant Writing: Your Junior Writing Partner

Throughout this book, you've seen AI quietly working alongside you—helping brainstorm ideas, organize data, tighten paragraphs, analyze rejections, and make your writing stronger.

Still, some grant writers worry they'll be replaced by AI. I did too, at first. But it didn't take me long to realize this is just another tool—one that only works with a human at the helm. AI cannot replace the heart and soul of your organization. It doesn't know your community, your mission, or your stories unless you tell it first. It's smart, but not strategic. Fast, but not thoughtful.

So, let me be clear: AI won't replace grant writers. But grant writers who know how to use AI may replace those who don't.

In this lesson, we'll pull back the curtain and show you how to use AI as your most efficient writing sidekick, without giving up your role as the head writer of your organization's story.

What AI Can Do

Think of AI as your junior grant assistant—fast, tireless, always available, but still needs guidance. When used well, it can:

- Identify potential grant funders by state as well as their funding priorities and giving history.
- Draft first versions of sections based on your notes.
- Rewrite dense or chopping copy into plain, clear language.

- Tighten wordy paragraphs to better meet character or word limits.
- Brainstorm proposal titles or headlines from your copy.
- Generate sample evaluation plans or SMART objectives from your input.
- Summarize long narratives into executive summaries.
- Identify missing elements or unclear responses in your draft.
- Format messy budget narratives, board lists, or bios into clean drafts.

#93: *Grant writing is a team sport.*
Grant writing is a team sport, even if the "team" is just the tools and resources you lean on. Use the tools at your disposal—whether it's software, AI, templates, or a trusted colleague—to brainstorm, draft, and tighten your copy.

What AI Can't Do

As powerful and helpful as AI is, it has limits. While AI can save time, spark ideas, and help you stay organized, it can't replace your human insight, relationships, or lived experience. Great grant writing is more than just stringing sentences together. It's about connection, trust, and heart. That's where your writing shines.

AI can't:

- Understand your unique funder relationships.
- Know the culture or history of your organization.
- Capture your emotional tone or lived experience.
- Spot political or local dynamics influencing decisions.
- Replace your ethical judgment or strategic instincts.
- Build real trust with funders, board members, or stakeholders.
- Create authentic, nuanced stories of your impact.

AI writes words. You build trust.

#94: *Psst. Don't tell AI I told you this, but it sometimes makes things up.*
Always double-check your data, outcomes, and names before hitting submit. Even AI admits it makes mistakes, so make sure your final draft reflects your accuracy, not its assumptions.

How to Build AI Into Your Grant Workflow

By now, you've seen what AI can do, and the *AI Pro Tips* in the book have likely sparked a few ideas of your own. The next step is knowing where and how to use it without disrupting your rhythm. The goal isn't to replace your process, but to streamline it. Use AI as a support tool that saves time, clears roadblocks, and lets you focus on strategy, relationships, and storytelling—the parts only *you* can do. The goal isn't to overhaul your entire process. It's to plug in AI where it saves you time and brainpower, without losing your voice or control.

Here is the AI reality check: AI is fast, not wise. It makes you faster, not smarter. It won't replace your judgment, your voice, or your strategy. You're still the lead writer. AI is just the assistant—helpful, tireless, and occasionally a little too confident, but only as good as your direction. Think of it this way: You're the head chef. AI is your sous chef—great at chopping vegetables, measuring ingredients, and cleaning up the mess. But only you know the recipe, the seasoning, and when it's ready to serve.

So don't fear it. Train it. Use it. With the right prompts and a little oversight, AI can help you spend less time stuck — and more time telling the powerful, fundable stories only you can write.

#46: ***The more specific your prompts, the better AI performs.***
Feed it real data, clear goals, and actual funder requirements. What you get out of it is only as good as what you put into it.

LESSON 19 Key Takeaways

- ☑ *AI helps with drafts, summaries, edits, and research—but don't let it be the main voice in your grant.*
- ☑ *Use AI to save time and polish your work, not to replace your thinking.*
- ☑ *Always give AI clear prompts, real data, and specific goals.*
- ☑ *Never submit AI-generated content without reviewing. It can make mistakes.*
- ☑ *Trust-building, storytelling, and strategic alignment? That's the human part of your grant, and your superpower.*

COMING UP NEXT In *Lesson 20*, we'll explore what's **Beyond Grants** and how to diversify your income streams and build multiple layers of fundraising to support your mission year-round.

Strong goals tell funders not just what you'll do, but why it matters and who will be better because of it.

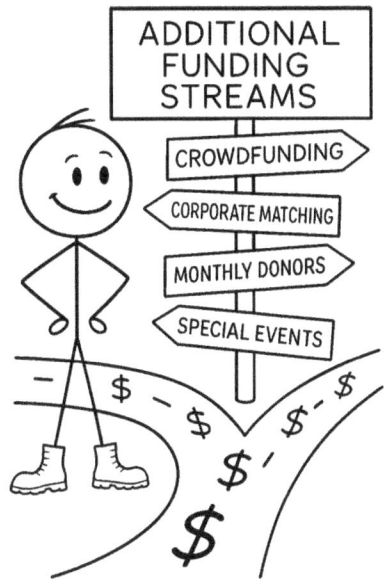

LESSON 20

Beyond Grants: Diversifying your Funding Streams

By now, you've done the hard part. You know how to research funders, write strong proposals, and build relationships with grantmakers. But here's a little secret: *Grant writing works even better when it's not your only funding tool.*

Strong organizations don't rely on one income stream. They build funding ecosystems. And the more diverse your income, the more attractive you are to funders. Why? Because it shows you're stable, supported, and smart about money.

Let's look at a few funding tools you can start adding to your fundraising strategies.

Crowdfunding

Use it to rally online donations for a specific need or project—from raising money for Fluffy's much-needed surgery to fixing the transport van. It's easy to launch, highly shareable, and brings in new donors when you need them most. Crowdfunding is like shooting up an emergency flair: bright, urgent, and built for attention.

▶ *Why It Packs a Punch:* Crowdfunding is simple to set up, spreads easily through social media, attracts donors outside your usual circle, and adds an emotional pull that compels people to give.

▶ *Where It Falls Flat:* It's not reliable for long-term funding, can lead to donor fatigue if overused, and only works if you have a strong story and can keep people updated.

#95: *Use crowdfunding to solve one clear problem.*
Tell a focused story, include great photos, and ride one big wave of support. Then close it out—and move on.

Peer-to-Peer Fundraising

Whether it's Facebook birthday fundraisers or Giving Tuesday challenges, peer-to-peer fundraising turns your volunteers, adopters, and fans into mini-ambassadors. Whether they're running a birthday campaign, hosting a dog walk, or just asking friends to donate, peer-to-peer fundraising helps spread your mission far and wide—without you having to do all the heavy lifting.

▶ *Why It Packs a Punch:* It shows strong community support, helps you build relationships with new donors, and the contributions can really add up over time.

▶ *Where It Falls Flat:* It requires motivation and support from your team, can be harder to track if done through third-party platforms, and tends to lose steam without clear goals or a little friendly competition.

#96: *Don't underestimate peer-to-peer campaigns.*
Peer-to-peer campaigns tap into your supporter's social networks—people you don't know or who don't know you. When your supporters take the lead, they lend their credibility to your cause. That kind of endorsement is worth more than just dollars.

Social Media Micro-Campaigns

You don't need a massive campaign to make a difference. A $10 Friday challenge, a short TikTok video celebrating a happy adoption, or a "sponsor-a-spay" story with a donate button can all spark engagement. Small "asks" paired with big reach can create powerful momentum, especially when shared widely.

▶ *Why It Packs a Punch:* Social media keeps your mission top-of-mind in a fast-moving world. It's easy to launch, easy to repeat, and ideal for engaging mobile donors who respond well to quick, emotional stories.

▶ *Where It Falls Flat:* Without creativity, your posts may disappear into the scroll. These campaigns often raise more awareness than dollars, and they require consistent content to stay effective over time.

#97: *Social media is for storytelling.*
Funders scroll too, so show them a mission that's alive, engaged, and making a difference. Every post is a chance to prove you're worth investing in.

Monthly Donors

Small monthly gifts—$10 here, $25 there—may not seem like much at first, but they create something rare in the nonprofit world: predictable, flexible income. These gifts often go unnoticed, but behind the scenes, they're keeping the lights on and the doors open.

▶ *Why It Packs a Punch:* It provides consistent and unrestricted funding, strengthens donor loyalty, and grows steadily over time.

▶ *Where It Falls Flat:* It takes time to build momentum, requires ongoing donor engagement, and can feel invisible if you're not regularly recognizing your supporters.

#98: *Monthly donors are like your own private grant program.*
No deadlines, no reports, just loyal, steady support. Make them feel special. These are the people funding your everyday mission, month after month.

Wish Lists and In-Kind Donations

In-kind donations—non-monetary gifts like pet food, cleaning supplies, or services—can help cover every day needs and stretch your budget. You can post a wish list on your website or use platforms like Amazon Wish Lists, Chewy Gives Back, or organize local supply drives. Sometimes, a bottle of bleach meets a more urgent need than a check.

▶ *Why It Packs a Punch:* This approach fills urgent supply gaps, gives supporters a different way to contribute, and helps reduce your spending in key areas. It's especially effective during specific campaigns or emergencies when people want to take immediate action.

▶ *Where It Falls Flat:* It won't help pay salaries or medical bills, and you may receive items you don't actually need. It also takes coordination; someone has to manage the lists, track deliveries, and thank donors.

#99: *In-kind donations = budget relief.*
Every item you don't have to buy, like bleach, paper towels, or pet food, frees up cash for the things you *can't* get donated, like staff salaries or vet bills. These donations may not feel glamorous, but they keep your operations running and your budget breathing. Don't underestimate the power of a well-stocked shelf.

Corporate Matching and Workplace Giving

Many companies offer to match donations or even volunteer hours but most employees don't realize these programs exist. A quick reminder to your supporters can turn one donation into two, with no extra cost to them. It's one of the easiest ways to boost giving with minimal effort.

▶ *Why It Packs a Punch:* It doubles individual donations, invites employer engagement, and is often an underused opportunity waiting to be tapped.

▶ *Where It Falls Flat:* It depends on employees knowing and using their benefits, requires clear instructions to follow through, and not all companies offer it.

#100: *Include a one-line reminder about corporate matching gifts in your thank-you emails.*
A quick note like "*Ask your employer if they'll match your gift!*" can turn one donation into two, at no extra cost to the donor.

Special Events (Virtual and In-Person)

From galas to trivia nights, special events bring people together and raise money at the same time. Virtual and hybrid formats help cut costs and widen your reach. Whether it's a formal fundraiser or a fun community gathering, events give supporters a reason to show up and give.

▶ *Why It Packs a Punch:* Events boost your visibility, deepen community connections, and offer donors a memorable, mission-driven experience. When thoughtfully planned, they can also generate significant unrestricted income that supports your broader goals.

▶ *Where It Falls Flat:* Events require considerable time, planning, and staff or volunteer support. Without a clear budget and goals, expenses can easily overshadow earnings. Plus, fundraising outcomes can vary year to year, making them less predictable than other revenue streams.

#101: *You don't need a ballroom to raise big bucks.*
A mission-focused event that's fun, heartfelt, and community-driven can wag more tails and win more hearts than a tuxedo ever could. Think dog washes, shelter sleepovers, trivia nights, or "Yappy Hours" at your local brewery. If it brings people and pets together, it can bring in donations too.

Thrift Stores

Operating a thrift store may not sound glamorous, but for many animal shelters, it's one of the most reliable and mission-aligned funding streams out there. Secondhand stores turn donated clothes, furniture, and household goods into steady income that supports lifesaving programs. Every purchase helps fund adoptions, medical care, and shelter operations—no grants or appeals required.

▶ *Why It Packs a Punch:* Thrift stores offer ongoing, unrestricted revenue and keep your shelter visible in the community. They also provide a place for supporters to give back in more ways than one—by donating items, shopping regularly, or volunteering their time.

▶ *Where It Falls Flat:* Running a store takes staff, space, and good management. You'll need to stay on top of inventory, pricing, and customer service. Without enough foot traffic or the right oversight, a thrift store can become a drain instead of a driver.

 **#102:** *A well-run thrift store isn't just a fundraiser—it's a billboard for your mission.*
Display adoptable pets, post program flyers, and create a feel-good shopping experience that turns every sale into a second chance for an animal. And don't forget: every donated couch, coffee mug, or vintage jacket is helping an animal in need. That's impact you can price and tag.

Direct Mail Appeals

Even in the digital age, a heartfelt letter still gets results, especially with older donors who appreciate something tangible and love receiving something in the mail. Seasonal appeals, holiday letters, or emergency mailers can spark donations and keep supporters engaged year-round.

▶ *Why It Packs a Punch:* It's personal, proven, and great for donor retention. Emotional stories paired with matching gifts can drive significant revenue.

▶ *Where It Falls Flat:* It takes time to craft, print, and mail. Younger donors may ignore it, and postage costs can add up fast if you don't have a targeted list.

 **#103:** *Use real stories and real names.*
The more your direct mail appeal like a letter from a friend—not a brochure—the better your results.

Major Gifts and Donor Cultivation

Big gifts don't come from cold asks. They come from relationships. When you invest time in stewarding your most loyal donors, you open the door to significant, unrestricted support.

▶ *Why It Packs a Punch:* Fewer donors, bigger dollars. These major gifts can fund programs, renovations, or emergency needs without tying your hands.

▶ *Where It Falls Flat:* It takes patience and a personal touch. There's no quick payoff, and relationship-building can't be automated.

 **#104: Don't wait for a capital campaign to start building major donor relationships.**
Send updates, make calls, and make them feel like part of your team.

Legacy Giving (Planned Gifts)

Planned gifts like bequests, retirement fund designations, or charitable trusts allow donors to support your mission beyond their lifetime—and often, they're easier to secure than you think. You don't need a lawyer on staff or a complicated campaign. Just start the conversation. Ask supporters to consider including your shelter in their will or estate plan, and give them simple sample language they can share with their advisor.

▶ *Why It Packs a Punch:* Legacy gifts are usually large, require no immediate cash, and help ensure your shelter's long-term sustainability.

▶ *Where It Falls Flat:* It takes years to see the impact, and many organizations avoid bringing it up—so donors never consider it.

 **#105: *Make these conversations a habit.***
Include a gentle legacy reminder in your thank-you notes, newsletters, and website. You're not asking for money, you're offering a way to make a lasting difference.

Adoption Sponsorships

Invite donors to "sponsor" the care of an adoptable animal or their spay/neuter. Whether they cover the full cost of medical care, food, or a waived adoption fee, it's a feel-good way to give—and a powerful connection point.

▶ *Why It Packs a Punch:* It turns a donation into a direct act of compassion. Donors love knowing exactly who they're helping.

▶ *Where It Falls Flat:* It takes coordination to match donations with animals and ensure timely updates. And without personalization, it can feel transactional.

#106: *Put a face to the cause.*
Sponsor Bella's adoption" is 10x more effective than "Give $75 to help a dog."

Retail Partnerships and Round-Up Campaigns

Partner with local businesses to collect donations at checkout, host adoption events, or launch a "round up for rescue" campaign. It's a low-effort ask for shoppers, but a high-impact way to raise awareness and funds.

▶ *Why It Packs a Punch:* It introduces your mission to new audiences, boosts community visibility, and adds up fast. Spare change can turn into thousands over time.

▶ *Where It Falls Flat:* It takes relationship-building, signage, and follow-up. Without consistent communication, donations can stall or never make it your way.

#107: *Treat your business partners like donors.*
Thank them publicly, feature them in social posts, and check in often. A little appreciation goes a long way and keeps the partnership strong.

Merchandise Sales

From custom T-shirts to mugs and tote bags, merchandise can raise funds while turning your supporters into walking ambassadors for your mission.

▶ *Why It Packs a Punch:* It builds brand awareness, offers a tangible connection to your cause, and can be low-risk with print-on-demand services.

▶ *Where It Falls Flat:* Managing inventory or upfront costs can be tricky. Without good design and promotion, items may sit unsold.

#108: *Tie it to your mission.*
A shirt with a real shelter pet or a message like *"Adopt, Don't Shop"* or *"Rescue is My Favorite Breed"* inspires action. Calendars featuring adopted animals, mugs with pets, or totes that say *"I Support Local Rescue"* turn everyday items into walking billboards for your cause.

How This All Supports Your Grants Program

By now, you've seen that fundraising isn't one-size-fits-all. From crowdfunding to merchandise sales, social media appeals to legacy giving, each strategy has its place, and its power. Some bring in cash fast. Others build long-term sustainability. Together, they form a fundraising ecosystem that supports your mission year-round.

But here's the key: These tools don't just raise money—they raise confidence. When funders look at your application, they're not just reading your story; they're reading your stability.

They want to know:

- Do other people support this mission?
- Will they survive if we don't fund them again?
- Are they scrappy, smart, and sustainable?

A strong fundraising mix answers yes to all three questions. It shows that you're not putting all your eggs in one basket. That you're creative and committed. That you're building a future for your organization.

#109: *Start with one new revenue stream.*
Test it. Track it. Tweak it. And most of all, tie it back to the animals.

#47: *Use AI to brainstorm new ideas.*
AI can help you brainstorm campaign themes, donor language, and even video scripts. Ask: *"Give me 10 ideas for a crowdfunding campaign for a cat rescue needing urgent medical funds."* You bring the heart; AI brings the headlines.

LESSON 20 Key Takeaways

- ☑ *Recognize that grants are powerful, but they're just one part of a broader fundraising strategy.*
- ☑ *Diversify your income to increase financial stability, flexibility, and funder appeal.*
- ☑ *Leverage crowdfunding to address urgent needs and share emotionally compelling stories.*

- ☑ *Empower supporters through peer-to-peer campaigns that expand your reach and credibility.*
- ☑ *Run social media micro-campaigns to build momentum through consistent, creative engagement.*
- ☑ *Grow a monthly donor base to create steady, unrestricted income you can count on.*
- ☑ *Use in-kind donations and wish lists to meet immediate needs and reduce expenses.*
- ☑ *Promote workplace giving and corporate matching to multiply the impact of every gift.*
- ☑ *Host virtual or in-person events to build community, visibility, and annual support.*
- ☑ *Operate thrift stores to generate ongoing, unrestricted revenue and raise local awareness.*
- ☑ *Cultivate major donors for transformational gifts that fund core programs and growth.*
- ☑ *Encourage legacy giving to ensure long-term sustainability through bequests and planned gifts.*
- ☑ *Offer adoption sponsorships to create personal giving opportunities tied to individual animals.*
- ☑ *Partner with local businesses for retail round-ups and co-branded campaigns that boost donations.*
- ☑ *Sell mission-aligned merchandise to turn supporters into walking ambassadors.*
- ☑ *Build your fundraising mix thoughtfully—layer by layer—for resilience and long-term success.*

COMING UP NEXT You did It! You've built your skills, sharpened your strategy, and powered through every chapter. This is your graduation moment. In *Lesson 21*, **Beyond Mission Ready**, we'll celebrate how far you've come, and what's next.

LESSON 21

Being Mission Ready: Celebrating Your Graduation Day (Minus the Cap and Gown)

Let's take a moment and talk about what just happened.

Whether you're a volunteer just trying to help your local shelter, or a staff member juggling grant writing with ten other hats, you made it through *Grant Writing Boot Camp for the Animal Advocate*.

You showed up, page after page. You stuck with it through **Project Narratives, Sustainability, Evaluation** and **Metrics**. And you came out on the other side stronger, clearer, and more confident.

My hope?

- That new grant writers feel confident tackling their first proposal.
- That seasoned pros found new ways to streamline, organize, and level-up their strategy.
- And that everyone — regardless of experience — walks away feeling more equipped, more empowered, and more ready to fund what matters.

Yes, it's a lot. But it's a full boot camp, and you've now got everything you need to be successful at grant writing.

You're not just someone who *hopes* they can write a grant – you *are* a grant writer now. A storyteller. A translator of impact. A project coordinator. A bridge between vision and funding.

You're the one behind the scenes, gathering the numbers, the need, and the everyday magic—and turning it into something funders can believe in.

That's not just a milestone—that's mission readiness.

Grant writing isn't just paperwork. It's advocacy. It's visibility. It's how we speak up for animals, for communities, and for the work that needs doing.

I've seen teams start from scratch with no experience, no systems – just heart. And you know what they did?

- They kept showing up.
- They tracked outcomes.
- They collected stories.
- They trained staff.
- They faced rejection – and they learned from it.

Eventually, they got their first grant. Then another. Not because they were lucky, but because they were prepared, persistent, and purpose-driven.

That's the work *you've* done here.

And here's the best part: You're not just writing grants anymore—*you're creating change*.

- For animal shelters doing heroic work with limited resources.
- For staff who are stretched thin but still show up.
- For volunteers who give their hearts, their time, and their weekends.
- For the animals who can't ask for help but need it all the same.

You write to fund what matters, give voice to the voiceless, support the people who make it happen, and give your mission the fuel to fly.

And here's the good news: once you've written a few grants, the process becomes surprisingly intuitive.

So, what's next? You graduate and celebrate!

Not with a cap and gown, but with something even better: the tools to write bold, compelling, fundable grants that make a difference.

Congratulations, graduate. Your mission starts now.

#110: Confidence doesn't come from writing one perfect grant. It comes from showing up prepared, curious, and committed with every grant application. That's how you grow your voice, your instincts, and your results. That's who you are now!

#48: Remember, AI is your assistant – not your replacement. You bring the heart, the insight, and the mission. AI helps you work faster, write smarter, and stay focused on what really matters. Want more ways to use it?

COMING UP NEXT After a brief P.S., you will find *Appendix 1*, How to Access Your All-in-One Grant Toolkit. In *Appendix 2*, you will find links to the 110 Boot Camp Tips, and in *Appendix 3*, you will find links to the 48 AI Pro Tips. Think of this as your grant writing gear bag—ready whenever you need a boost, a shortcut, or a sanity-saver. Because when the pressure's on, the right tools help you show up strong, clear, and fundable.

A QUICK P.S.

Wait! There's More!

Share What You Learned with Your Team.

If this book gave you clarity, confidence, or even just the courage to try—mission accomplished. You've seen what it takes to write great grants. Now help your team see it too. Share these lessons with your boss, your board, and your coworkers.

Most people don't realize what really goes into grant writing. They think it's just filling out a form and asking for money.

"Can you write a grant for $50,000 for our medical program?"

"Sure. What exactly do you need it for?"

"You know... medical stuff. Surgeries."

Until they understand the strategy behind the story, data, outcomes, and evaluation, they'll keep expecting you to perform miracles from vague ideas. And vague ideas don't win grants.

Help your team learn what tight, fundable, mission-driven proposals look like. Teach them what they need to know to help you write better grants.

Next, May I Ask You a Favor?

If this book helped you, I would love it if you would leave a quick review. You can post one on my website or wherever you purchased the book. Reviews help other animal advocates discover this resource and learn how they can make a difference.

Finally, Let's Stay Connected.

Thank you for letting me be part of your journey. If I can support you along the way, please don't hesitate to reach out. Whether you have a question I didn't cover or just need someone to say, "*You're on the right track*" — I'm *here*.

Find me on LinkedIn at **linkedin.com/in/cathyrosenthal**.

You can also visit **cathyrosenthal.com** for upcoming workshops, one-on-one consulting, and a full library of the downloadable tools, checklists, worksheets, and guides from the Appendix — all designed to make your grant writing easier, faster, and more successful. I didn't just want to teach you — I wanted to set you up with everything you needed to put these skills into action.

Whether you're a grant writer by title or the staff member, volunteer, or executive director who bravely said, "*I'll figure it out*", you don't have to do it alone. You've got a partner in this work — someone who believes in your mission and your ability to fund it.

You've juggled deadlines, data, a barking dog, and probably a cat on your keyboard — and still found a way to make magic.

You've got this! And I'll be cheering you on every step of the way!

Appendices

Grants are not gifts; they are investments. Show funders the return they can expect in lives saved and communities strengthened.

APPENDIX 1

How to Access Your All-in-One Grant Toolkit

Congratulations on taking the next step in your grant-writing journey! Now it's time to put what you've learned into action with my All-in-One Grantwriting Toolkit—the behind-the-scenes support that makes grant writing faster, easier, and more successful.

In the All-in-One Grant Writing Toolkit, you'll find:

- **Checklists** to keep you on track.
- **Templates** to save hours of work.
- **Worksheets** to spark fresh ideas.
- **A full sample grant** to show you exactly how everything fits together.

Whether you want to jumpstart a brand-new grant, plan a campaign, or find inspiration on a tight deadline, this toolkit gives you everything you need in one place. No more starting from scratch—just clear, ready-to-use tools to help you work smarter and feel confident about every application you submit.

How to Get Your Toolkit

Visit **CathyRosenthal.com/grantwritingbook** to find out how to access your digital grant writing toolkit and start using it right away.

The strongest proposals leave funders saying, "I can't imagine this community without this work."

APPENDIX 2

Links to the 110 Boot Camp Tips

16	**#1:** Create a digital folder.
17	**#2:** Define your need.
17	**#3:** Avoid animal welfare lingo.
18	**#4:** Don't wait until a grant opens to start crunching numbers.
19	**#5:** Listen to your clients.
19	**#6:** Stay focused on mission, not money.
20	**#7:** Make story collection a team sport.
22	**#8:** Show, don't tell.
22	**#9:** Pair **Stories** with **Data**.
23	**#10:** Start with what you are doing already.
24	**#11:** Do a readiness check before you start writing the grant.
26	**#12:** Match your needs with the grant type.
27	**#13:** Develop your funding pitch.
32	**#14:** Match projects with the right funders.
32	**#15:** Subscribe to federal and state grant bulletins.
33	**#16:** Network with the people who support you.

33	**#17:** Relationships build grants long before you apply.
34	**#18:** Don't overlook corporate funders in your own backyard.
35	**#19:** Size your ask strategically.
36	**#20:** When in doubt, talk to the funder.
36	**#21:** Write a one-sentence alignment test before you begin.
36	**#22:** Double-check their geographic funding area.
37	**#23:** Check average grant sizes before you determine your ask.
37	**#24:** Past giving tells you what the funder really supports.
37	**#25:** Dig into part XV of the 990 for funder priorities.
38	**#26:** Don't miss deadlines.
40	**#27:** Create a "No for Now" folder.
40	**#28:** Budget time in YOUR schedule for grant prospecting.
44	**#29:** Add a few extra columns for "Funder Fit," "Next Steps," and "Last Contacted."
44	**#30:** Your Grant Spreadsheet doesn't need to be fancy—it needs to be usable.
47	**#31:** Keep it real, not promotional.
48	**#32:** Your mission is the throughline.
49	**#33:** Build your master history.
49	**#34:** Mastering word and character counts.
54	**#35:** Show the need, loud and clear.
54	**#36:** Use local data whenever possible.
55	**#37:** Show funders what you see every day.
58	**#38:** The Core Six questions—and remove everything after that.
61	**#39:** Be crystal clear.
62	**#40:** Avoid vague language.
62	**#41:** The more specific you are, the stronger your narrative becomes.
63	**Boot Camp Sidebar:** 6 Tips for All-Volunteer Organizations

Appendix 2

66	**#42:** Don't overthink the executive summary.
68	**#43:** If your **Objective** starts with "We want to help…," try reframing it.
69	**Boot Camp Sidebar:** Tips for Writing a Strong **Goal**
70	**#44:** One clear sentence = one clear goal.
70	**#45:** Objectives should fit the goal—and prove it.
70	**#46:** When funders ask for "common goals," they're looking for shared purpose.
71	**#47:** Don't overload your proposal with too many **Objectives**.
72	**#48:** Write SMART objectives for your project goal.
74	**#49:** Start big to see all the angles—then edit down.
75	**#50:** Always write two to three SMART objectives funders can measure, even for general support.
79	**#51:** Want More **Stories**? Teach, Model, Celebrate.
79	**#52:** Don't wait until the end of the year to collect stories and stats.
81	**#53:** Don't overthink the formula. Just pair one story with one strong statistic.
84	**#54:** Know who you're helping and why they need your program.
85	**#55:** Remember, funders love data.
86	**#56:** Local Data = Local Credibility.
87	**Boot Camp Sidebar:** Pulling It All Together
89	**#57:** Say who, say why, say what's at stake.
89	**#58:** Prove you know your audience.
94	**#59:** Avoid vague language.
94	**#60:** Show them you got this.
94	**#61:** Write the plan, then follow the map.
96	**#62:** Show you are ready to roll.
96	**#63:** Plans change. Build in breathing room.
97	**Boot Camp Sidebar:** When Funders Ask for **Implementation** and **Timeline** Together.

98	**#64:** Match the details with the dollars.
103	**#65:** When in doubt, remember this.
105	**#66:** Don't try to predict the future—just show them you're paying attention.
105	**#67:** Build your own Metrics library.
106	**#68:** Write the report before you need it.
111	**#69:** Sustainability is a mix of resources, not a single source.
112	**#70:** A mix of revenue sources shows you're thinking strategically.
112	**#71:** Don't write your Sustainability plan like a wish list.
113	**Boot Camp Sidebar:** Can You Raise Money on Social Media or GoFundMe?
114	**#72:** Structure your appeal as a story.
114	**#73:** Crowdfunding is a tool, not a strategy.
116	**#74:** Fresh eyes may find what you miss.
121	**#75:** Your Cover Letter is the voice-over for your proposal
124	**#76:** Your **Supporting Documents** send a message to funders.
125	**#77:** Don't let the project budget be an afterthought.
126	**Boot Camp Sidebar:** What's a Budget Narrative—and Why Do Funders Care?
126	**#78:** Don't skip the story behind the numbers.
127	**#79:** Keep short bios in your digital folder.
128	**#80:** Create one master "Grant Attachments File" in your digital folder.
130	**#81:** Set a "safety deadline" that's at least 48 hours before the real one.
131	**#82:** Funders remember good manners.
132	**#83: Rejection** doesn't mean your program isn't strong.
137	**#84:** Track every **Rejection** in your **Grant Spreadsheet**—and the reason why, if you can figure it out.
139	**#85:** Still think the funder's a good fit?
142	**#86:** Print your original grant and highlight every promise.

142	**#87:** What if things aren't going to plan?
143	**#88:** As soon as your grant is approved, mark the report deadline on your calendar.
144	**#89:** Remember that digital folder you created?
144	**#90:** Keep your funders—and your team—in the loop.
144	**#91:** Don't disappear after the check clears.
145	**Boot Camp Sidebar:** Do I Need a Relationship with the Funder?
145	**#92:** If the door's open, step in.
148	**#93:** Grant writing is a team sport.
148	**#94:** Psst. Don't tell AI I told you this, but it sometimes makes things up.
152	**#95:** Use crowdfunding to solve one clear problem.
152	**#96:** Don't underestimate peer-to-peer campaigns.
153	**#97:** Social media is for storytelling.
153	**#98:** Monthly donors are like your own private grant program.
154	**#99:** In-kind donations = budget relief.
154	**#100:** Include a one-line reminder about corporate matching gifts in your thank-you emails.
155	**#101:** You don't need a ballroom to raise big bucks.
156	**#102:** A well-run thrift store isn't just a fundraiser—it's a billboard for your mission.
156	**#103:** Use real stories and real names.
157	**#104:** Don't wait for a capital campaign to start building major donor relationships.
157	**#105:** Make these conversations a habit.
158	**#106:** Put a face to the cause.
158	**#107:** Treat your business partners like donors.
158	**#108:** Tie it to your mission.
159	**#109:** Start with one new revenue stream.
163	**#110:** Confidence doesn't come from writing one perfect grant.

As a grant writer, you are the storyteller, the translator of impact, and the bridge between vision and funding—turning numbers, needs, and everyday magic into something funders can believe in.

APPENDIX 3

Links to the 48 AI Pro Tips

18	#1: Let AI be your editor.
20	#2: Summarize your biggest program successes.
22	#3: Turn raw data into talking points.
23	#4: Use AI to rank your projects.
26	#5: Let AI help you research funders.
26	#6: Draft short summaries for each project.
28	#7: Let AI help you spot weaknesses.
32	#8: Not sure which grants platform is right for you?
32	#9: Let AI save you time.
32	#10: Let AI do the sorting.
35	#11: Turn tax forms into actionable intelligence.
36	#12: Use AI to spot geographic patterns.
39	#13: Use AI to reframe your ask through a funder's eyes.
39	#14: Let AI sort and prioritize your funder list.
39	#15: Use AI for a second opinion.

39	#16: Speed up your research with AI summaries and comparisons.
39	#17: Use AI to summarize key dates from 990 forms.
40	#18: Use AI to run a funder risk check.
45	#19: Let AI help you analyze your **Organization's History**.
50	#20: Need a tighter version of your **Organization's History**?
55	#21: Use AI to strengthen your **Needs Statement**.
63	#22: Writer's block? Let AI get you started.
66	#23: Unsure where to start your executive summary?
72	#24: Struggling with vague goals?
74	#25: Ask AI to condense your long-form **Goals** and **Objectives** into a grant-ready summary.
81	#26: Make sure your story and your stats work together.
81	#27: Paste **Stories** and **Data** into AI and ask…
86	#28: AI can help you with research.
86	#29: Let AI do the heavy lifting.
89	#30: Use AI to find and format local demographics.
89	#31: First, write long. Then edit for space.
95	#32: Need an **Implementation Plan**? Let AI help.
97	#33: Let AI spot gaps to keep you in sync.
98	#34: Let AI help you trim copy without losing meaning.
103	#35: Use AI to strengthen your **Evaluation** section.
106	#36: Use these AI prompts to help you draft or refine your **Evaluation** and **Metrics** section.
113	#37: Here are some great AI Prompts to help draft strong Sustainability answers.
114	#38: Let AI draft your appeal, then edit to make it your own.
116	#39: Let AI be your final gut check, not your ghostwriter.

121	#40:	Draft your Cover Letter, then ask AI to improve.
128	#41:	Use AI to clean and polish attachments.
130	#42:	Use AI for one last polish.
137	#43:	Use AI to help analyze what might have gone wrong.
139	#44:	Let AI be your post-game replay
144	#45:	AI is your reporting and editorial assistant.
149	#46:	The more specific your prompts, the better AI performs.
159	#47:	Use AI to brainstorm new ideas.
163	#48:	Remember, AI is your assistant—not your replacement.

Funders don't just read proposals; they imagine the future you're promising. Make it vivid.

APPENDIX 4

Sample Grant

Bringing Mobile Pet Vaccine Clinics to Underserved Communities

Mission

The mission of the Compassion Pet Care Alliance (CPCA) is to reduce pet overpopulation and keep pets healthy and in their homes by providing high-quality, affordable spay/neuter surgeries and preventative wellness services for owned pets. Since 20XX, CPCA has worked to remove barriers to veterinary care by operating three stationary high-volume spay/neuter clinic and a mobile unit that delivers vaccines, microchips, and surgical scheduling directly to neighborhoods where families face the greatest challenges accessing care.

Every day, our staff and volunteers meet pet owners who love their animals deeply, but lack the resources or access to keep them healthy. Our role is to bridge that gap by ensuring that basic veterinary services—spay/neuter, vaccinations, and microchipping—are available, affordable, and delivered in ways that meet families where they are.

Organizational History

Founded in 20XX, CPCA launched in response to a growing need for affordable spay/neuter services in financially challenged neighborhoods. At that time, many pet owners were calling city shelters or surrendering pets because they simply could not access basic veterinary care. We opened our first high-volume spay/neuter clinic with a focus on prevention—helping families keep their pets healthy and reducing the number of unwanted litters entering the shelter system.

As the need grew, so did CPCA. We have since expanded to **three stationary clinics**, each located in underserved areas, ensuring families have more access points for affordable spay/neuter and wellness services. By 20XX, we recognized that even with multiple clinics, transportation and cost remained barriers for many pet owners. In response, we launched our mobile unit, bringing core vaccines, microchips, and on-site spay/neuter scheduling directly into neighborhoods with the highest need. In 20XX, we took another step forward by creating a dedicated transport program, which picks up pets from communities facing the steepest access barriers and brings them safely to our clinics for surgery. This program ensures that lack of transportation never forces a family to forgo essential veterinary care for their pets.

When the COVID-19 pandemic disrupted veterinary services nationwide, CPCA adapted quickly. We maintained safe operations, continued performing surgeries and hosting clinics, and emerged as a resilient, trusted partner for families who depend on us.

Since inception, CPCA has:

- Performed more than 145,000 spay/neuter surgeries for owned pets.
- Vaccinated and microchipped over 147,000 dogs and cats.
- Hosted 90 mobile clinics that reached families who otherwise would have gone without care.
- Transported more than 32,000 dogs and cats through our transport program to receive surgeries at our clinics.

Today, CPCA combines its three stationary clinics, mobile outreach, and transport program to form a comprehensive access-to-care model that reduces shelter intake, promotes responsible pet ownership, and improves the health and well-being of pets across 16 counties.

Executive Summary

We are requesting $50,000 to fund 10 mobile vaccine clinics over the next 12 months. These clinics will be hosted in five targeted ZIP codes identified by city shelter data as producing some of the highest numbers of owner surrenders, stray intakes, and reported dog bites. We also identify ZIP codes that are financially challenged through census.gov and city-data.com. Each ZIP code will receive two clinics, reaching a combined total of 1,000 owned pets (approximately 100 pets per clinic).

At every clinic, families will receive core vaccinations and microchips for their pets, while also being given immediate opportunities to schedule spay/neuter surgeries at CPCA's stationary clinic. Services will be offered at no cost, supported by bilingual staff, with evening and weekend scheduling to increase accessibility.

By focusing on prevention and access, the project aims to achieve a 20% reduction in city shelter intake from these ZIP codes over a 12-month period compared with the previous year's baseline.

This proposal directly advances the foundation's goals of equity and access (removing barriers to care), animal protection (preventing disease and overpopulation), and community (strengthening families and neighborhoods through local partnerships).

Boot Camp Notes
Executive summaries are not requested very often. They are simply summaries of your proposed program.

Project Narrative

When Maria brought her two dogs to a CPCA vaccine clinic, we were hosting it in her neighborhood at a nearby community center. Neither of her dogs had ever been seen by a veterinarian before. That day, they received their core vaccines and microchips, and Maria left with confirmed spay/neuter appointments for both dogs—something she was grateful for as her pair of dogs had already had three litters.

Stories like Maria's illustrate why mobile access matters. Many families in the five targeted ZIP codes delay or forego routine veterinary care because of cost of care (which we cover through grants and donations), transportation, and the simple absence of a nearby provider. These barriers increase the risk of preventable diseases, accidental litters, and ultimately higher intake at the city shelter when those litters need homes.

The proposed 10 clinics will directly counter these barriers by providing:

- **Preventative care:** Vaccinations and microchips for 1,000 owned dogs and cats.
- **Spay/neuter scheduling:** On-site bookings for pets not yet sterilized, supported by reminders and transportation referrals.
- **Education and Resources:** Bilingual information on pet care, disease prevention, and resources.
- **Convenience:** Evening and weekend events hosted at trusted community locations.

With two clinics per ZIP code, families will have both an initial opportunity for care and a follow-up option for boosters or missed appointments. This two-touch model increases compliance, builds trust, and ensures better outcomes for pets and their families.

Common Goals / Alignment

CPCA's mobile vaccine clinics align directly with the foundation's three priority areas:

▶ *Equity and Access.* We eliminate structural barriers by bringing services directly into high-need neighborhoods. Bilingual staff, no-cost services, and local clinic locations ensure that care is within reach for every family, regardless of income or transportation barriers.

▶ *Animal Protection.* Vaccines prevent the spread of contagious diseases, microchips increase reunification, and spay/neuter prevents unwanted litters that lead to shelter intake.

These interventions protect individual pets and strengthen the overall health of the community's animal population.

▶ *Community.* By partnering with schools, food banks, community centers, and local leaders, we embed our services where families already gather, ensuring both accessibility and trust.

Together, these strategies will serve 1,000 owned pets and help reduce city shelter intake from the five targeted ZIP codes by 20% in the next 12 months.

Target Audience

The project serves pet-owning households in five high-need ZIP codes: 76115, 76104, 76105, 76110, and 76119. These areas were identified by city shelter data as generating some of the highest rates of surrenders, strays, and dog bites.

Families in these neighborhoods face multiple overlapping barriers:

- High poverty rates (20% to 27% vs. 14% statewide).
- Predominantly minority populations (60 to 80% African American or Hispanic).
- High renter occupancy (55% to 85%).
- Limited vehicle access (15% to 20% of households are without a car).

These factors mean many pets never receive core vaccinations, remain unsterilized, and are at risk of not only having multiple litters of puppies and kittens, but also being surrendered when families cannot manage medical costs associated with pregnancies. By offering mobile, no-cost services where they live, CPCA removes these barriers and empowers families to keep their pets healthy and at home.

Demographics

Example: ZIP Code 76115

- Population: ~34,000 residents, ~11,800 households.
- Poverty rate: 23% (vs. 14% statewide).
- Renter occupancy: ~62%.
- Households without a vehicle: ~18%.
- Majority-minority population: ~74% (56% Hispanic, 13% African American, 20% other/multiracial).
- Median household income: ~$48,000 for a family of four.

Similar conditions exist in the other four target ZIP codes, where poverty ranges from 20% to 27% and transportation limitations affect up to one in five households. These indicators highlight why mobile delivery is essential—traditional clinics are simply inaccessible for many families.

Boot Camp Notes
In your grant, please provide this information for ALL 5 ZIP codes or provide a range or average of these numbers so all ZIP codes are represented.

Program Objectives

The objectives of this project are to:

1. Host 10 mobile vaccine clinics (two in each of five targeted ZIP codes) over 12 months, serving approximately 1,000 pets.

2. Provide preventative care to pets with the goal of reaching at least 70% first-time veterinary visits.

3. Convert at least 90% of unaltered pets into scheduled spay/neuter surgeries through on-site booking.

4. Achieve a 20% reduction in city shelter intake from the five targeted ZIP codes within 12 months—equivalent to 250 fewer dogs and cats—based on the 1,250 pets surrendered from these areas in the previous year.

5. Reduce preventable disease among pets entering shelters by improving upstream vaccination coverage by 50%. (In the previous year, more than 500 dogs and cats entered the shelter from these ZIP codes unvaccinated.)

Implementation Plan

CPCA will execute the program through a structured plan:

1. **Targeting:** Confirm ZIP codes using shelter intake data, census.gov and city-data.com.

2. **Site selection:** Secure clinic sites at trusted community hubs (schools, food banks, recreation centers).

3. **Outreach:** Conduct bilingual promotions using flyers, social media, community newsletters, and door hangers.
4. **Clinic operations:** Each event staffed by a veterinarian, two veterinary technicians, and bilingual customer service staff. Services include vaccines, microchips, and on-site surgery scheduling. Clinics offered during evenings/weekends to maximize attendance.
5. **Follow-up:** SMS and phone reminders at 72h/24h before appointments; transportation referrals to our transport vehicle to reduce no-shows.
6. **Quality and safety:** All vaccines stored and administered per veterinary guidelines; incident response protocols in place.
7. **Monitoring:** Attendance, services delivered, and bookings tracked in clinic logs and scheduling software for future reporting.

Evaluation / Outcome Measures

CPCA will evaluate success through both outputs and outcomes:

▶ *Outputs:*

- 10 clinics hosted.
- 1,000 pets vaccinated and microchipped.
- 90% of the pets who are unsterilized scheduled for their spay/neuter surgeries.

▶ *Outcomes:*

- 20% reduction in city shelter intake from the five ZIP codes (measured against the prior year baseline).
- Increased vaccination coverage in neighborhoods with historically low access.
- Reduced disease outbreaks in the city shelter from unvaccinated animals entering the shelter.

▶ *Data sources:* Clinic records (vaccines, chips, surgeries scheduled) and quarterly shelter intake data by ZIP.

▶ *Data reporting:* Monthly clinic reporting, quarterly intake analysis, and annual comprehensive evaluation.

Collaboration

Collaboration is essential to this project. CPCA will partner with:

- City Animal Services for intake data and cross-promotion.

- Local food banks and schools to host clinics and provide outreach.
- Homeowners and tenant associations to build trust and encourage attendance.
- Other animal welfare groups to co-host mega-events that combine vaccinations with pet food, supplies, and additional pet care resources.

These partnerships extend our reach, reduce costs through in-kind contributions, and ensure that services are culturally and geographically accessible.

Boot Camp Notes
This is a great place to list your community partners by name—if the foundation already knows or respects them, that recognition strengthens your case.

Project Program Background

CPCA is a spay/neuter and preventative care organization committed to breaking down barriers to veterinary services. Our focus is keeping pets in homes by providing affordable spay/neuter surgeries and preventative wellness care. Over the past decade, CPCA has become a regional leader in reducing shelter intake and improving community pet health.

Key accomplishments:

- 145,000+ spay/neuter surgeries for owned pets.
- 147,000+ vaccinations and microchips provided.
- Mobile vaccine program launched in 20XX, reaching more than 32,000 pets in underserved neighborhoods.

Our unique combination of stationary clinic capacity, mobile outreach, and proven follow-up systems positions CPCA to deliver this project successfully and to achieve the measurable reduction in shelter intake outlined in our objectives.

Timeline (12 Months)

▶ *Q1 (Jan–Mar):* Conduct outreach and planning with community partners, city council representatives, and neighborhood groups. Launch the first two clinics (one in each of two targeted ZIP codes). Collect baseline data on attendance and spay/neuter bookings.

▶ *Q2 (Apr–Jun):* Hold three additional clinics to ensure every ZIP code has been served at least once. Midyear evaluation of turnout, vaccine uptake, and surgery scheduling rates;

adjust outreach methods (e.g., door hangers, bilingual flyers, text reminders), if participation is lower than expected.

▶ *Q3 (Jul–Sep):* Host three more clinics, including booster vaccinations where needed for pets from earlier clinics. Expand transportation support for families without reliable access. Begin comparing shelter intake data against baseline for early impact indicators.

▶ *Q4 (Oct–Dec):* Conduct the final two clinics to complete the 10-clinic cycle (two per ZIP code). Carry out a comprehensive evaluation of all clinics, compile data on total pets vaccinated, microchipped, and scheduled for spay/neuter, and compare against shelter intake numbers. Submit final report and outcomes to funders, stakeholders, and community partners.

Sustainability

Each clinic costs approximately $5,000. This grant request covers all 10 clinics ($50,000 total). To ensure continuity beyond this funding period, CPCA will:

- Apply for continued foundation support and explore government funding opportunities.
- Seek corporate sponsorships (pet retailers, logistics companies, grocery chains) for clinic underwriting.
- Cultivate individual donors through campaigns showcasing clinic impact stories.
- Leverage in-kind contributions (venues, volunteer veterinarians, donated supplies).
- Explore limited fee-for-service add-ons for families able to pay something, like a $20 co-pay, reinvesting grant monies into the free program.

This diversified funding strategy will ensure the program's long-term viability and expand its reach in future years.

Communication / Dissemination

CPCA will keep stakeholders, funders, and the community informed through:

- Quarterly progress reports and stakeholder meetings.
- Grant reports with outcomes, financials, and impact stories.
- Community outreach via bilingual social media posts, newsletters, and press releases.
- Donor recognition through appreciation events, spotlights, and signage at clinics.

By sharing both data and human stories, we will demonstrate transparency, impact, and gratitude for the support.

Budget Narrative

Total Project Cost: $50,000 (10 clinics)

Estimated Costs:

- Vaccines: $10 per dose × 3,000 doses = $30,000
- Microchips: $5 each × 1,000 = $5,000
- Staff/tech hours: $1,000 per clinic × 10 = $10,000
- Fuel/transport: $200 per clinic × 10 = $2,000
- Supplies/consumables: $300 per clinic × 10 = $3,000

Total: $50,000

In-kind contributions, such as donated venue space and volunteer support, further leverage resources and reduce costs.

Other Grant Attachments

Funders often request additional attachments to accompany your proposal. Many of these are standard—such as your 501(c)(3) letter, board list, and most recent 990—while others provide valuable context about your organization's capacity, impact, and readiness to deliver on the project. Together, these documents enhance the credibility of your application and give funders confidence in both your stability and your ability to succeed.

▶ *Board of Directors List:* A document listing the names, positions, affiliations, and (when possible) terms of service for all members of the organization's board of directors. Funders review this to understand governance, community representation, and leadership stability.

▶ *Organizational Chart/Biographies of Key Personnel:* A visual representation of the organization's structure, showing hierarchy and reporting relationships. Include resumes or bios for key staff, board members, and consultants involved in the project. Funders look for strong leadership, clear accountability, and staff with the expertise to deliver the proposed work.

▶ *Strategic Plan:* A document outlining the organization's mission, vision, goals, and strategies for the next three to five years. Funders want to see that your work is part of a larger, intentional roadmap and not a stand-alone activity. A current strategic plan signals stability and forward planning.

▶ *Partnership Agreements:* Formal agreements or MOUs with partner organizations, outlining roles and terms of collaboration. Funders view signed agreements as proof that partnerships are active, reliable, and not just "in name only."

▶ *Letters of Support or Endorsement:* Letters from individuals, partner organizations, or community leaders endorsing your work. The strongest letters highlight what the partner will contribute (space, volunteers, referrals) and the outcomes expected. Funders use these to validate community buy-in.

▶ *Marketing and Communication Materials:* Examples of brochures, flyers, website pages, or social media content that promote your programs. Funders often scan these to see how you present yourself to the public and whether your messaging aligns with the project you're proposing.

▶ *Photos:* High-quality images of your programs, staff, volunteers, and clients (with permission). Funders sometimes use these in their own reports or publications, but more importantly, photos help them visualize your impact and humanize your story.

▶ *Client Success Stories or Testimonials:* Short stories or quotes from clients that illustrate the difference your services make. Funders like to see both data and human outcomes; testimonials show the lived experience behind the numbers.

▶ *501(c)3 IRS Determination Letter:* Your official IRS letter confirming tax-exempt nonprofit status. This is required for eligibility with most foundations and serves as proof of your legal standing.

▶ *Most Recent 990:* Your most recent IRS Form 990, which outlines your mission, programs, and financials for the year. Funders check this for financial transparency, consistency with your proposal, and to see other sources of support.

▶ *Financials:* Your most recent independent audit report, or if you don't have one, your most recent profit and loss statement, balance sheet, and year-to-date financials. Funders use this to assess your fiscal health and your capacity to manage grant funds responsibly.

▶ *List of Funders for Previous Year or Up to Three Years:* A list of foundations, corporations, government agencies, and individuals who have supported your work, along with amounts. Funders often review this to see who else is backing you and to gauge whether your funding base is broad and stable.

▶ *Operational Budget:* A detailed annual budget showing projected revenues and expenses for the entire organization. Funders want to see the full financial picture to understand how their grant fits into your overall operations.

▶ *Project Budget:* A detailed budget specific to the proposed project, outlining revenues and expenses tied to that work. Funders expect this to align precisely with your narrative and objectives, and they often compare it line by line with your budget narrative.

▶ *Funding for the Project to Date:* A list of all funding already secured for this project, including donors, grants, and amounts. Funders use this to assess momentum (who else has invested) and to ensure their grant will be leveraged effectively rather than filling the entire budget alone.

www.ingramcontent.com/pod-product-compliance
Lightning Source LLC
Chambersburg PA
CBHW061211230426
43665CB00032B/2982